TOWARD A U
HUMAN 1

MW00425991

John Mark Reynolds

University Press of America,® Inc.
Lanham · Boulder · New York · Toronto · Oxford

To Deborah Modrak and Al Geier

Contents

CHAPTER 1: PLATO'S PSYCHOLOGY AND THE TIMAEUS   *1*

Toward a Unified Platonic Psychology   **1**

Tejera and Strauss on Plato   **3**

The *Timaeus* as Myth   **7**

The Strong-Myth Commentators   **10**

The Weak-Myth Platonists   **16**

A.E. Taylor   **23**

Reading the *Timaeus*   **30**

CHAPTER 2: THE PSYCHOLOGY OF THE TIMAEUS   *47*

The Opening Platonic Moves   **47**

Reason in the Soul: Historical and Philosophic Considerations **52**

Implications of the Cosmic Soul for Human Psychology   **55**

The Cosmic Soul and Simplicity   **58**

The Cosmic Soul: Simplicity and Mixture   **60**

The Problem of Motion in the Simple Soul   **62**

Cosmic Soul: Some Final Reflections   **68**

Time and the Soul   **69**

The Creation of a Unified Human Soul   **74**

The Soul and Body Relationship 79

Introduction to the Problem 79

Necessity and the Relationship of Body and Soul 80

Relationships within the Parts of the Human: Motion in the Soul/Body Composite 82

The Body and Soul: A New Element 89

The Mortal Soul: Creation and Function 90

The Location and Function of the Mortal Soul 90

Divination in the Mortal Soul 92

Problems for the Platonic Soul 97

Overview 97

The Problem of Individuation 99

Status of the Account of the Creation of the Body 101

The Soul at the Moment of Death 104

Plato's Views on "Science" Relation to His Psychology 108

Animals and the Human 112

Psychological Dualism 118

Introduction to the Issues 118

Plato and Substance Dualism 118

The World of Becoming: the Nature of Soul and Matter 119

Motion, Soul, and Matter 121

Humanity and Dualism 124

Death and Memory 125

Conclusion: Plato's View of the Human Soul 129

**CHAPTER 3: THE SOUL IMMORTAL AND POLITICAL: THE
PSYCHOLOGY OF TIMAEUS APPLIED TO THE PHAEDO AND
THE REPUBLIC**   *141*

Immortality: the Psychology of the *Phaedo*   142

Phaedo and the Issue of Consistency   142

Light from the *Timaeus* on the Psychology of the *Phaedo* 147

The Soul of the City: The Psychology of the *Republic*   150

The *Republic's* and the *Timaeus'* Psychology: Do They
Compliment Each Other?   150

The Human Soul in the City Revealed in the Cosmology of the
Timaeus   154

Concluding Remarks   157

Bibliography   163

Index   171

Preface

How should one read older books? That is a more difficult question than many seem to think. There are many candidates for the "correct" method in the academy of the early twenty-first century. Some might think the correct method is to (1) search through the older book for ideological error. This reinforces ideologies, but presupposes that older books are unable to challenge contemporary cultural prejudices. A person might also read the text with the single goal of (2) discovering what the book said to the first readers. This sociological reading would also have value for learning more about the people and culture from which a book first came. Another type of reading sometimes favored is to (3) simply read the book to see what it means to the reader. The book stimulates personal thoughts that might in the end have no connection to the original intent of the author. Such a reader might believe that escaping one's own world-view is impossible, or that such originality leads to interesting results.

This book represents another sort of interaction with the text. Plato believes in timeless truth. Is he correct? If so, the works of Plato are worth examining to see if they illuminate problems in philosophy and human culture that have a timeless quality. One way of determining if this is so would be to assume the *potential* truth of Platonism, seeing what could be made of it. This sort of reading of a text has a long and honored tradition. The question motivating this interaction is: "What if the text has some timeless truth that Plato intended to convey through his dialogues?" Behind this question is the foundational attitude of seeking and submitting to truth.

My argument is not that this is the only way to read the text.

Some will find such a project "old fashioned," an attitude C.S. Lewis described as "chronological snobbery." Charity to a thinker seems to demand that sometimes one pause and see if his thoughts can be put together in this manner. After all, it could be that Plato was forward thinking enough to have anticipated many things that only later have become obvious.

Assuming that Plato may have had insight into deep and timeless truths, I want to begin with the text and work views out from it. Though confident I owe a great debt to many more contemporary writers like Leo Strauss, A.E. Taylor, and Alfred Geier, my goal has not been to interact with their views of Plato. This sort of scholarly interaction is valuable. However, it often moves one away from the text and understanding Plato to understanding the secondary author. My goal was to attempt to interact with the text as directly as possible. In this sense, I am following in the footsteps of scholars such as Leo Strauss. At the same time, I do not reject the methodological attempt at clarity of arguments in writers like Vlastos.

Persons hoping to find a "post-modern" or sociological account of Plato will not find it here. Nor is this book an attempt to exhaustively catalogue a booming contemporary discussion of *Timaeus*. This book does not treat the text as cultural artifact, but as a living work of philosophy. My training is in analytic philosophy and my first concern is to see what can be understood from the text in that tradition. However, I am not interested in generating arguments that are separate from the text itself. My hope is that all the arguments I advance in this book are arguments that Plato intended or would have intended to make given certain contemporary problems in philosophy.

Critics have suggested that Plato has no consistent, fully developed human psychology. I argue that a full and consistent Platonic view of the human soul does exist within the Platonic canon and that the key to finding it is in the dialogue *Timaeus*. This human psychology is of interest to philosophy because it is not Cartesian dualism, but neither is it any of the modern forms of materialism. Philosophy is not as safely in the grip of materialistic accounts of personality as it may be thought to be. Other options that do not require a "ghost in the machine" or "man as merely machine" should at least get a hearing.

First, I defend *Timaeus* from attempts by some commentators such as A.E. Taylor to claim the dialogue does not contain Platonic doctrines. Taylor argued that the *Timaeus* was a sort of Platonic experiment: a conflation of Empedoclean and Pythagorean science to which Plato would not have been committed. To the contrary, such a view is implausible given ancient understandings of the texts, especially that of Aristotle. Moreover, scholars such as Leo Strauss and Victorino Tejera have suggested that any list of Platonic doctrines is necessarily suspect. Though there is much to admire in the ways of reading texts suggested by Strauss and Tejera that has influenced this work, I dissent from the view that Platonic doctrines cannot be discovered and known.

Second, the text of the *Timaeus* is examined in order to expose and interpret the human psychology found within it. The human soul is the potential for circular motion when it comes into contact with appropriate matter, such as the fire found in stars. This motion is confused by contact with inappropriate matter. The human soul does not exist in a state separate from a body for any length of time. Examining the human soul also allows a better understanding of the cosmic soul Plato postulates in Timaeus.

Finally, I briefly compare the psychology found in *Timaeus* to the views of the human soul found in *Phaedo* and *Republic*. From this examination, I conclude that Plato develops the idea of soul as a bridge between the world of perfect being and the visible world of eternal becoming. The human soul is circular motion of the "same" which can be imparted to appropriate matter. This motion is rational, thus allowing the soul to be the seat of cognition. Plato's psychology must ultimately picture the human soul as having an accidental simplicity and thus a non-essential immortality. These tools, developed independent of concerns about other areas of Platonism, allow problems in the canon to be solved. For example, certain seeming inconsistencies in Plato's psychology admit solution. Arguments for immortality are strengthened by being clarified by this new view of Plato's psychology.

Plato also has developed a psychology that allows for the soul to have the appearance of priority in order of creation without having an actual first moment of creation. The implications of his psychology on his ethics, his view of the animal world, and theology are examined. The psychology developed from *Timaeus* resolves difficulties that are alleged to occur in the accounts of the soul found in both *Phaedo* and the *Republic*.

These are tentative conclusions coming at the end of a decade of reflection, mostly on the text of Plato. I am all too aware of the

xii   Preface

presumption of reaching such conclusions after such a short period of time. Plato is a profound writer who often hides his meaning behind difficult images. The pleasure of wrestling with such a subtle mind compensates for any difficulties. My hope is that these first fruits will stimulate other and better thoughts in my students, in me, and in others who care for Plato.

Acknowledgments

This book is a revision of my doctoral dissertation at the University of Rochester, 1996. I would like to thank Fieldstead and Company for the support necessary to continue my research into Plato's psychology. I would also like to thank J.P. Moreland for arranging a private grant that allowed for the final revision time needed. Jessica Snell and Adam Johnson provided invaluable assistance in preparing the manuscript for publication. Jessica and Adam have been some of the best reasons to keep pursuing Truth.

CHAPTER 1: PLATO'S PSYCHOLOGY AND THE *TIMAEUS*

Toward a Unified Platonic Psychology

Plato presents a unified, coherent, and philosophically interesting account of the human soul. As with any complex vision of human psychology, this presentation has not been without critics. Some do not see the Platonic psychology as consistent or helpful to Platonic philosophy.[1] In contrast to these criticisms, I argue that Plato's view of the soul has great philosophic merit and internal consistency. Furthermore, I claim that the dialogue *Timaeus* is the key to resolving alleged difficulties in Plato's view of the soul. Once these difficulties are resolved, Plato's psychology can be examined to see if it offers helpful insights to contemporary philosophers.

This book is written by a philosopher working in the analytic philosophical tradition. I assume that Platonic psychology may have more than historical interest to the reader. My goal is to give to Plato's writings the same charity in interpretation that would be granted to a contemporary philosopher. This book is not concerned with more "post-modern" ways of reading texts. On the other hand, I am sensitive to the criticisms of Strauss and others that analytic philosophers have looked first to analytic philosophers and only later at the text of Plato. I work as the chairmen for a growing department committed to doing learning in the tradition of Strauss and others like him. Therefore, this work is deeply indebted to the model of scholarship proposed by Leo work is deeply indebted to the model of scholarship proposed by Leo Strauss, even when it departs from some of his most important conclusions about how to read ancient texts, particularly Plato. Where I have done so, I have tried to justify such a move. Analytic philosophers owe Strauss a debt for reminding them of the importance of a close examination of the text. However, the tools of analytic philosophy and its ways of reading texts are sometimes too lightly dismissed by those in the Strauss camp.

I have tried to look at Plato's psychology by starting from the Platonic canon itself. While I have consulted scores of more recent papers, they have not been the focus of my research. Using the motivation to return to the text provided by Strauss, with the guidance of traditional commentators like Proclus and Aristotle, the goal was to see what Plato was saying in the text. I hope to have written a work that can act as a modest contribution to the school of commentators exemplified by A.E. Taylor and Francis Cornford.

How shall I proceed? First, I will show that the *Timaeus*, a dialogue around which some controversy swirls, contains descriptions of the soul that Plato intends the reader to take as his own views. I must also prove that Plato wants us to take the views given in *Timaeus* regarding the soul as his ultimate position on the topic. Second, a consistent exposition of the psychology of the *Timaeus* must be worked out. Third, this psychology must be consistent with the view of the soul argued for in the other Platonic dialogues. Fourth, the Platonic psychology developed should be helpful in addressing some criticisms advanced regarding Plato's view of the soul. Finally, I will suggest that Plato's psychology may be valuable in contemporary psychology. These five tasks will form the framework for this discussion.

Fundamentally, Plato believed the soul to be circular motion. I will show that this Platonic doctrine about the soul is a consistent development of Greek psychology before the time of the Academy. Plato believed that this natural circular motion made the soul capable of reason. Plato uses his idea of soul as a conceptual middle between the Forms, in what he will call the World of Being, and the visible world, which he will call the world of Becoming.

The human soul shares in the intellectual ability of soul in general, because it too is best described as circular motion. The human soul has two major parts: the immortal part and the mortal part. Only the immortal part, strictly speaking, is soul in the full sense. The immortal part shares in the basic characteristic of soul in general: circular motion. The immortal part, found in the head region of the human, can have its motions confused in conjunction with the mortal soul and the body, but it never loses its natural tendency to move in a circle. The immortal human soul has a type of simplicity that allows for an accidental immortality.

The mortal human soul is divided into two parts. As a lesser creation of demigods, the mortal soul is somewhat like the immortal soul in terms of material composition, but not like it in terms of essential nature or attributes. This difference, due to impurities in the substance making up the mortal soul, allows for a gradation in the makeup of the cosmos from the Forms to visible matter. One moves, in terms of being, from the absolute being of the Forms, through the immortal soul which has accidental immortality, to the mortal soul which can undergo change and death, to matter which is necessarily constantly changing. This picture of the human soul will have demonstrable impact on how one understands a number of issues in Plato. Plato's views on immortality, the ethical status of animals, the nature of science, evil, and the composition of matter will all be illuminated by this description of his *Timaeus* psychology.

These doctrines of human psychology presented in *Timaeus* will also be helpful in dealing with textual difficulties often found by philosophers in the psychology of *Phaedo* and *Republic*. In *Phaedo*, I will argue that this psychology saves the cyclical argument for immortality from at least one difficult problem. In *Republic,* Plato will no longer face questions about the compatibility of the *Timaeus* psychology and the *Republic* psychology. The correct formulation of the psychology of the *Timaeus* will be the key to a proper understanding of the Platonic psychology.

Tejera and Strauss on Plato

Several commentators[2] have advanced reasons for rejecting the *Timaeus* as an expression of Platonic opinion. Others have accepted this same dialogue as Plato's mature views on the subject.[3] The controversy over how to read the dialogues has split philosophers into three major camps. The first group rejects the notion that any dialogue should be used to reflect on the material found in any other dialogue.[4] Some members of this school of thought also feel that to construct any

Platonic doctrines is foreign to the whole spirit of the Platonic enterprise.[5]

The second group holds that it is, perhaps, possible to develop broad Platonic doctrines, but that the *Timaeus* is the wrong dialogue in which to look for them. These persons include those who think that the *Timaeus* itself is merely a myth (though other dialogues contain "serious" Platonic notions)[6] and those who think the *Timaeus* is a cosmological experiment.[7] In either case, to take the details of the story of Timaeus as being critical to the understanding of Platonism would be dangerous or foolhardy.

The third group, which includes most of the ancients (including Aristotle, Proclus, and Plutarch), takes the *Timaeus* to be a serious and important work in understanding Platonic psychology and doctrines.[8] Some modern readers like Gregory Vlastos have accepted the notion of the *Timaeus* as myth. This follows Plato's own description of the dialogue in *Timaeus* 29d. These commentators wish to read the dialogue somewhat differently than the ancients.[9] These modern readers make this exegetical shift without challenging the ancients' main assumption that the dialogue gives an account Plato means us to read as his serious views on the subjects it presents. I will argue that the first view is most probably mistaken and that the second and third views are compatible with my general project.

In the book *Plato's Dialogues One By One: A Structural Approach*, Tejera argues cogently for the first view of the *Timaeus*. He believes that the establishment of Platonic "doctrines" is foreign to the spirit of the dialogues.[10] He also asserts that the dialogue is best understood in an "ironic" spirit. Plato is a philosopher who "... plays with whole theories and whole systems."[11]

Tejera and other interpretations in this tradition,[12] give several reasons for believing that the formation of Platonic doctrines from the dialogues is unwise. Tejera sums up his case against developing "doctrines" from Plato by giving the expositor of such generalizations four challenges. First the doctrinal reader

> will have to prove (independently of unproved assumptions about the dialogues) that the speaker from whom he got the answers is (i) speaking for Plato and (ii) that Plato meant them literally, or in the same sense as himself. He would have to prove that a speaker in another dialogue who gives a contradictory answer is (iii) not speaking for Plato. Such a reader would also have to accept that (iv)

this speaker also meant the abstracted words literally – otherwise the doctrinal reader can't trust his proof that the first reader was speaking literally.[13]

What can be made of this challenge? He would have us read the dialogues in isolation, except in those rare instances where the dialogues themselves refer to each other. It is not clear, however, that the burden of proof is actually on Tejera's doctrinal reader.[14]

First, Tejera wants the doctrinal reader to "prove" that the person being referenced in a particular dialogue is expressing Plato's views. On the surface, there is much to commend this argument on the supposed ambiguity regarding who is speaking for Plato. It is certain that Plato never speaks in his own voice. Speakers in the dialogues range from an unnamed Athenian (e.g. the *Laws*), to Socrates, to other Greeks (such as Timaeus). Which speaker represents the views of Plato?

An easy solution would be to say the primary expositor always represents the Platonic point of view. Tejera might question how the reader knows the interlocutor does not represent Plato's view in the dialogue. To support this hesitancy in identification, Tejera could point out that in dialogues like the *Parmenides*, it is not clear whose point of view is being expressed by the primary speaker. The views traditionally considered Platonic are sometimes expressed by an interlocutor in this dialogue. Who is speaking for Plato in *Parmenides* and the other such dialogues?

This is not as easy a question to answer as one might think. Socrates is the best candidate for the voice of Plato in the dialogues. Socrates, however, does not appear in every dialogue. He is not present, for example, in the *Laws*. Plato does not then universally speak through Socrates. One could claim that when Socrates is present in a dialogue that he represents the views of Plato. When he is not present, some other interpretive principle must be brought into play. This weaker claim, however, presents the commentator with difficulties of its own. What about dialogues where Socrates is present, but does not carry the weight of the conversation? Who then speaks for Plato? *Parmenides* is an excellent example of a dialogue where commentators do not agree regarding this issue.[15]

I do not think, however, that this criticism need long detain the careful reader of Plato. While it is the case that the dialogues do not directly state who is speaking for Plato, if indeed anyone is speaking for Plato in the dialogues, there are sufficient reasons to assign a very high probability to certain positions. First, while the dialogues are silent about who is speaking for Plato, Aristotle is not. Aristotle, as Plato's most important student, would be in the best position to know how Plato thought about his own dialogues (He would certainly be in a better position than a critic in the late twentieth or early twenty-first centuries). Aristotle frequently quotes a speaker in a dialogue and attributes the views mentioned to Plato. For example, in *Physics,* Aristotle writes, "This is why Plato in the *Timaeus* says...."[16] There are numerous other examples of this in Aristotle's work.

What does this "prove"? First, it does not prove, in the strongest sense, that Plato actually meant a particular statement to be taken as his own views. Minimally, it is the case that Aristotle could be mistaken in this attribution. Second, Aristotle is not always a charitable commentator on persons with whom he disagrees. It does, however, seem to place the burden of proof on Tejera. While Aristotle might be viewed as distorting some Platonic doctrine (for reasons of his own), it is difficult to see how he expected to profitably attribute to Plato views that were not Plato's own one generation after Plato himself was alive. Once again, this does not close off the possibility that Aristotle might do such a thing, it merely places the burden of proof on Tejera. It is a burden of proof that he can never meet.

Why do I say this? Tejera is arguing from silence. The strength of the argument rests in what Plato does not say. Tejera does not deduce his position from any positive claim in the text. If, therefore, the burden of proof is shifted to Tejera and those in his camp, it is impossible for them to respond.

Of course, Tejera could claim that the literary form of dialogue itself lends credence to his point of view. This is, at best, suspiciously like a circular argument. Where does one find the information that tells what Plato meant to do when he chose to write in dialogues? It is clear from the writings of his chief student, Aristotle, that it was at least possible to believe that he was placing Platonic doctrines in them. Tejera should, following his own style of reasoning, suspend judgment on what this literary genre signified until the texts themselves (or the witness of Plato in other works) answer the question. This, of course, Tejera fails to do. Instead, he assumes that he knows what the literary form of dialogue signifies. This in the face of the fact that such knowledge escaped Aristotle.

The more traditional reader may, on the other hand, with perfect consistency follow the lead of Proclus and Aristotle and search carefully through the dialogues for the doctrines that Plato wished to develop. She may develop a working theory about how to determine when it is that we are hearing Plato's voice in a particular dialogue. Then, when such a theory has been developed, she may examine that theory in the light of all the dialogues, against the witness of those philosophers closest in time to Plato, and with broadly established notions of exegesis found in philosophy. One example of such an exegetical rule might be the principle of charity.[17]

Finally, if consistently applied, Tejera's arguments are self-referentially incoherent. How does the reader of Tejera know that Tejera himself is not writing ironically? Tejera in his text does not say that he is not writing ironically.[18] In the text he says, "In other words, that irony has occurred is always disputable."[19] Of course, the context and force of the book itself would leave the burden of proof on the person who claimed that Tejera was being satirically Straussian in his book on the Platonic dialogues. What would Tejera have gained in writing this way? In the same way, given historical evidence[20] and the fact that philosophers have believed that they have found many fairly consistent doctrines in the dialogues forcefully argued for by Plato (for example, the theory of recollection in the *Meno*), Tejera must provide some positive evidence of such widespread irony in Plato. To say that it could exist is not enough, for the same could be argued about any work, including Tejera's.

Timaeus might contain a doctrinal key to understanding the Platonic psychology. Tejera's challenge to this notion has been successfully met. There is a second group of philosophers who present a more formidable barrier to my thesis. They see the *Timaeus* as pure myth or a mere cosmological experiment not to be taken as expressing Plato's doctrinal views.

The *Timaeus* as Myth

In his book *Preface to Plato*, Eric Havelock says,

> The *Timaeus* is Plato's final tribute to this kind of speculative vision. But it is a vision, not an argument. Dare we suggest that in the

> *Timaeus*, for this very reason, he also accomplished the final betrayal
> of the dialectic, the betrayal of that Socratic methodos which had
> sought for formulae in order to replace the visual story by the purely
> abstract equation?[21]

Havelock writes that the *Timaeus* is full of "mythology" and that for
this reason the dialogue became the favorite reading of philosophers of
the Middle Ages.[22] For Havelock, the *Timaeus* is not a place to look for
Plato's thought at its finest, let alone for the key to Platonic
psychology.

Those philosophers that would agree with Havelock in saying
that the *Timaeus* is merely an elaborate myth[23] can point to several
interesting lines of argument. They can find great textual support for
their claims, which I will detail shortly.

What are the arguments of Havelock and those who agree with
him? The first centers on the person of Timaeus. Timaeus is a
mysterious and shadowy figure. He is not Socrates and, in fact, is
speaking to Socrates.[24] If one is to assume, as I did in arguing against
the Tejera-Strauss style critic, that Socrates usually speaks for Plato,
then perhaps one should assume that Timaeus is not expressing the
views of Plato. Nothing is known of Timaeus' background. It is not
even known whether he was an actual person.[25]

These strong-myth commentators do not stop with questioning
the status of Timaeus himself. They develop several further lines of
argument.[26] The implications of these arguments vary widely in terms
of their impact on my general argument. Those of F.M. Cornford, for
example, support the notion that *Timaeus* is a myth. As such, they have
been used by strong-myth commentators. Cornford is not a strong-myth
commentator himself. He does present their arguments, however, in
their most persuasive form.

What is a strong-myth commentator? I take a strong-myth
commentator to be one who holds that Plato was committed to none the
details of his creation myth, *Timaeus*. Strong-myth commentators are
divided about Plato's motivation for writing such a dialogue. Taylor
views it as a kind of cosmic joke. Havelock sees it as a deliberate
betrayal of Plato's better instincts. It is not my intention to criticize the
notion that *Timaeus* is a myth. I am certainly not challenging the
strong-myth commentators on this central point. However, what does
Plato mean by "myth"?

The question is what the term μῦθος meant to Plato in writing the *Timaeus*. Does it mean, as the strong-myth commentators suggest, that Plato is not committed to the details within the dialogue? Such a view would be fatal to my approach. It will be adequate for my purposes if the *Timaeus* is read as a myth in a weaker sense proposed by Cornford. Cornford's weak-myth approach concedes that the *Timaeus* is a myth, while allowing some ideas in it to be taken as serious expositions of Plato's mature and considered opinions. Of course, the supporters of both the weak-myth and the strong-myth approach make many of the same arguments. Do the weak-myth Platonists draw the correct conclusions from those arguments?

F.M. Cornford, in *Plato's Cosmology,* pins much of his arguments regarding the status of the dialogue in Plato's thought to Timaeus' own description of his account as a "likely fable" [εἰκότα μῦθον].[27] Cornford believes that this account is a myth (his translation) in two respects. First, "no account of the material world can ever amount to an exact and self-consistent statement of unchangeable truth."[28] The world of Becoming   would never submit to exact description.

Second, Cornford points out that the story is a cosmogony not unlike that of Hesiod and other early Greek cosmologists. "Such a story was, to Plato, very far from being like the truth."[29] The universe unfolds in time. For Plato a more serious account would be descriptive. Such a descriptive and non-mythic exploration of the cosmos would surely be impossible in a Platonic world-view. The universe is not the sort of place about which Socrates can ask his, "What is . . .?" question. It simply would not hold still long enough to allow such precise characterization. The telling of a story [μῦθος] that holds the creation of the universe up to the reader's view is the surest sign, according to Cornford, that Plato is storytelling.

This is similar to the point that Havelock made in the earlier quotation from *Preface to Plato.* Havelock and Cornford are thus united in seeing Plato as being less than committed to the all the details of the *Timaeus*. Havelock and the strong-myth group take these Cornford-style arguments further and see a negative break with the doctrines and practices of other Platonic dialogues. Cornford departs from Havelock in believing that despite an "irreducible element of poetry" these views can be mined for Platonic points of view in answering cosmological questions. Both groups center their ideas

around these three central arguments: Timaeus is a questionable figure
to stand in for Plato, Timaeus describes his own work as a μῦθος, and
the account is in a less than a serious style.

There is, therefore, a school of thought regarding the *Timaeus*
that, either strongly or in a weaker manner, finds the essential concept
for understanding the *Timaeus'* status in the Platonic corpus to center in
μῦθος (myth). What impact does this case have on my argument that
the *Timaeus* contains the key to unlocking difficulties in the Platonic
psychology? The position of Havelock, that the *Timaeus* is a betrayal of
the other dialogues, has little merit. I believe this can be easily
demonstrated. The arguments cited by Cornford support a weak-myth
position, but they fail to support the stronger claims of Havelock. From
this general condemnation I would exempt the rather unique case made
by the strong-myth commentator A.E. Taylor. His case is so different
from that of other strong-myth Platonists that I will comment on his
arguments in a separate section. In the end, I will argue that it too fails
to establish a strong-myth view of the dialogue.

The Cornford, or weak-myth position, in most forms, would
not be fatal to my point of view, even if adopted. Cornford believes that
the *Timaeus* contains some Platonic doctrines. I will demonstrate that
even Cornford should accept the Platonic psychology of the *Timaeus* as
being unquestionably Plato's own psychology.

More importantly, I will propose a third way of viewing the
μῦθος of *Timaeus*. This way will develop a positive argument for
reading *Timaeus* as the key to the Platonic understanding of
psychology. It is not enough in a positive sense for me to argue that my
view is possible, given all objections, Cornford's or others. The weak-
myth Platonist might agree that one could find Plato's doctrines in the
dialogue by carefully comparing it to the other writings. The other
dialogues could be used to weed the μῦθος out so that the pure
doctrines could be examined. My claim is much stronger. I must also
show why the *Timaeus* should be seen as the paradigm for Platonic
psychology.

While examining all these positions, it is important not to
forget that an entirely different way is also available: the clear witness
of Aristotle and Plutarch to a tradition of treating the opinions of
Timaeus as being synonymous with the opinions of Plato.[30] This
literalist view is clearly in harmony with deriving Platonic points of
view from the text of *Timaeus*. It could even be developed further to

show that *Timaeus* should be viewed as Plato's fullest and best expressions of his views on the human soul.

The Strong-Myth Commentators

I will begin by dealing with the claims made by Havelock and the strong-mythologizers. Their arguments, which were more fully explicated above, can be summarized as:

1. Timaeus does not speak for Plato. He is an unknown person historically, intentionally chosen to reveal that Plato is not giving his own views in the dialogue.
2. Timaeus himself describes his account as μῦθος (myth).
3. The account itself is in the style of Hesiod or other ancient cosmologists. Plato normally despises such story telling.

The first argument in the list is crucial to the strong-myth position. It is the one argument not used by commentators like Cornford (the weak-myth group). If it holds, then the *Timaeus* cannot be used as the key to Plato's psychology. However, the argument regarding the status of *Timaeus* is not nearly as compelling as it seems to be on first glance.

Plato usually chooses to speak through the person of Socrates. This point has already been conceded to the strong-mythologizer. It is not self-evident that Plato always does so, however. The *Laws* are one excellent example of this. Nor is Socrates always the main speaker when present in a dialogue, as *Parmenides* demonstrates.[31] In that dialogue Plato allows Parmenides to dominate the inquiry. It is at least arguable that he allows this for the same reason that he might have done so in the *Timaeus*. *Timaeus* may present a tentative Platonic proposal. The *Parmenides* is challenging a central Platonic idea. Platonic roles of a tentative or destructive nature may be assigned to some person other than Socrates. Socrates was primarily assigned the work of the dialectic. This means that dialogue from persons other than Socrates could be expressive of Plato's state of mind at the time of the dialogue. It could be seen as his best δόξα (opinion) regarding a particularly troublesome question.

Why should the reader believe that any given views are Plato's own in a dialogue? What means can be used to judge the matter as one reads? One needs an exegetical technique that is not just as an ad hoc explanation to enable a commentator to maintain his or her particular views.

I believe that four basic principles are sufficient to place the burden of proof on the critic who argues that Timaeus is not speaking for Plato. Since these were obliquely referred to when I was dealing with the Tejera-Strauss critique, I will only briefly mention them.

First, one can assume that if a speaker is in general harmony with the views common to the other dialogues then he or she has a high probability of being a person speaking for Plato.[32] Second, if Socrates is the main speaker in the dialogue, there should be a tendency to look for Plato's views in the doctrines he seems to support. Third, Aristotle should be viewed as a key source in knowing which general points of view should be attributed to Plato.[33] Finally, the main speaker in any dialogue is most likely to represent the Platonic point of view. This is particularly the case if Socrates is present and seems to affirm the views of the long-winded speaker.

I believe each of these exegetical assumptions are reasonable. In cases where:

1. Socrates is the main speaker.
2. Platonic doctrines are affirmed by the dialogue's main speaker.
3. Aristotle quotes the dialogue as containing Plato's own views.

a high degree of certainty should be attached to the doctrines derived from the dialogue. In cases like the *Timaeus*, where Socrates is not the main speaker, a reasonably high level of trust in the Platonic status of doctrines extracted from the dialogue can still be maintained if the other conditions are met.

The *Timaeus* is rife with examples of Timaeus supporting Platonic doctrines. To prevent any potential for circularity, I will not even mention the generally close accounts of the soul in the *Timaeus* and other dialogues. The dialogue consistently supports, and indeed undergirds, the theory of recollection and the theory of the Forms. It also provides an empirical basis for the Socratic aphorism that "no one does wrong knowingly." These are key, even central, Platonic concepts and Timaeus consistently argues for them, though of course he expands on them. If Timaeus is not Plato, it is difficult to imagine a more Platonic cosmologist. In fixing the date of composition of the *Timaeus*, many commentators who argue for an earlier date for the dialogue do so in part because of the affirmation of Platonic doctrine, especially the Forms, in it. Perhaps it is best to say that Plato's best portrait of himself as a cosmologist is found in the man Timaeus.

The dialogue *Timaeus* supports the theory of recollection by providing a biological account of how forgetfullness of the Forms comes to the human soul. Timaeus does this at 43b. Here he describes the soul as becoming ἀλόγος (without reason). This state is caused by the six contrary motions of the physical world. By suggesting how to bring these motions under control, Timaeus also provides a physical mechanism for recollection.

The *Timaeus* undergirds the theory of the Forms at every turn. It attempts to describe the interaction of the Forms with the Plato's real world (the world of Becoming). In beginning his discussion at 29a, Timaeus describes the universe as being created after the pattern of the eternal Forms. The universe is made "in the likeness of that Model," the Forms. The Forms are described, in traditional Platonic terms, as existent always and apprehensible by thought and reason.[34]

In its conclusion, the *Timaeus* gives a quasi-medical explanation for the fact that people who should know better do things that harm their souls and bodies. In Desmond Lee's translation, Timaeus says, "... no one wishes to be bad, but a bad man is bad because of some flaw in his physical make-up and failure in his education, neither of which he likes or chooses."[35] Plato explains evil actions as being due to certain physical illnesses that impact the soul via its connection to the body.

If it is granted that the views of Timaeus are the views of Plato, then why is Timaeus such a shadowy figure? Why not some better known character? For example, Parmenides was well known and respected. Timaeus' inclusion is not, however, so very different than the use of the Athenian stranger in the *Laws*.[36] The Athenian of the *Laws*, who does not even have a name, is an example of a mysterious person who presumably speaks for Plato. Even a Straussian like Thomas L. Pangle believes that good reasons can be given for the failure of Plato to use the mouth of Socrates in the *Laws*. He even proceeds to attribute certain views of the Athenian stranger to Socrates![37] The use of such a person to express what appears to be Platonic views would, therefore, not be unique to the *Timaeus*. No one knows the identity of the Athenian stranger. No one even knows if such a person existed, or if he was a composite drawn from Plato's imagination. In like manner, no one knows the status of Timaeus.

I believe, however, that there is a good positive reason for such a blank-slate sort of thinker in the context of the *Timaeus*. First, according to Critias, Timaeus gets to speak because he is the best astronomer. For Plato, this is a highly significant occupation. It is noteworthy that chief descriptions of this role outside of the *Timaeus* are found in *Republic*, which is inextricably linked to the *Timaeus* through the prefatory recapitulation of the *Republic* in *Timaeus*. Socrates in *Republic* says:

> And will not a true astronomer have the same feeling when he looks at the movements of the stars? Will he not think that heaven and the things in heaven are framed by the Creator of them in the most perfect manner? But he will never imagine that the proportions of night and day, or of both to the month, or of the month to the year, or of the stars to these and to one another, and any other things that are material and visible can also be eternal and subject to no deviation – that would be absurd; and it is equally absurd to take so much pains in investigating their exact truth.[38]

The astronomer, as the one who studies the motion of the heavens, gazes at things framed in the "most perfect manner." These are not, however, the eternal Forms about which true knowledge is possible. They are the most perfect objects possible in this world. They know the least deviation, but they remain visible and material and so are subject to change. They cannot be objects of true knowledge, but they are very close. They are closer than any other material thing. Timaeus, as an astronomer, may be viewed as the person best able to see whatever can be known of the origin and composition of the material world. He cannot, by the very nature of his subject matter, have perfect knowledge, but in the area of his specialty at least he can come as close as is possible.

It is also mportant to note that Socrates warns against trying to find the "exact truth" of astronomical relations. That does not mean that astronomy should not be studied, Socrates urges the proto-philosophers to this pursuit later in the *Republic*. It does mean that what moderns would call scientific or exact knowledge is not to be found in astronomy. This makes the use of the word μῦθος (myth) much more understandable. Timaeus cannot give the reader an exact account of the cosmos. A "likely story" is the best account the reader has a right to expect from the astronomer. In fact, it would be foolish for Timaeus to waste his time trying to do any better.

Plato in *Republic* 500c uses an astronomical metaphor to describe the work of the philosopher. The philosopher gazes at the eternal realities. In doing so Socrates says, "Θείῳ δὴ καὶ κοσμίῳ ὅ γε φιλόσοφος ὁμιλῶν κόσμιός καὶ θεῖος ἐις τὸ δυνατὸν ἀνθρώπῳ γίγνεται" (Ordered and divine is the philosopher having intercourse with the ordered and the divine, unto the power in humans to become such). The philosopher becomes as divine as she can be, by gazing at the "eternal and unchanging" order. This world of the Forms is not that of the celestial spheres. The celestial spheres are the closest paradigm in the visible world. She could come the closest to initiating a philosophical state of mind by meditating on astronomical data. Just as the city, which is larger than the human, becomes the means to see the nature of the soul in the *Republic*, so too the heavens, which are larger than the city, aid in seeing the nature of the Forms and the soul in the *Timaeus*.

Why then an unknown astronomer? Why not a better known figure or name (A prime contender for the position might be the astute Parmenides in the dialogue *Parmenides*)? First, any well known astronomer would commit Plato to a particular cosmology. This would severely restrict where the λόγος (account) could take the dialogue. By picking an unknown, Plato could construct his likely story without the constraint of any developed doctrines or school. Plato is clearly not happy with earlier philosophical speculations. To pick a proponent of one such school would be to make the *Timaeus* an absurdity. In fact, this is one of the strongest arguments that Plato intends the reader to take the cosmology of the *Timaeus* seriously. If Plato had picked some well known cosmologist to expound his "joke," then his comments about such projects in other dialogues would have made clear his intent.

Of course, it is not even certain that Timaeus was an unknown figure. Much knowledge of ancient cosmology and those who developed it has been lost to the modern reader over the years.

Cornford points out that a spurious dialogue (*On the Soul of the World and Nature*) was attributed to Timaeus in the first century.[39] Cornford considers it an obvious forgery. I do not dispute this fact. One may raise the possibility, however, that this dialogue may have been concocted, not just on the basis of Plato's dialogue, but on a richer tradition. Everyone who commented on this question in the ancient world believed there was a cosmologist named Timaeus. This speculation proves nothing, but it does point to the nature of Cornford's statement, "Timaeus is an unknown figure in history." He is certainly unknown to moderns; it is not known whether such a person existed in ancient times. Given the unsettled and incomplete status of modern knowledge about this area of Greek thought, this argument cannot weigh too heavily either way in the argument over the status of the *Timaeus*.

Finally, one should not disregard Socrates' comments regarding Timaeus in the dialogue itself. He refers to Timaeus as one who has reached the highest levels of philosophy at *Timaeus* 19c3. This is high praise, indeed. A skeptic might argue that Socrates is often cynical in his praise of sophists in the dialogues. Indeed in *Lesser Hippias*, assuming it to be an authentic dialogue, Socrates says at 368 that the good astronomer is the one who will best be able to speak falsely about such matters.[40] I must point out, however, that unlike the other dialogues in which an actual sophist appears, there is no Socratic exposure of Timaeus as a fraud in the dialogue. Hippias, for example, is revealed to be ignorant and insufferably pompous in *Lesser Hippias*. There is no such interrogation of Timaeus. In fact at *Timaeus* 19e, Timaeus and all those present are excluded from the ranks of the sophists. All things being equal, therefore, the prudent reader is left to accept Socrates' words of praise at their face value.

The other arguments presented by the strong-myth readers of *Timaeus* are also used by the camp that I have described as the weak-myth Platonists. As a result, I will deal with the remaining arguments traditionally advanced by both camps in the section concerned with the weak-myth Platonists.

The Weak-Myth Platonists

The Cornford reader rightly emphasizes the importance of a passage at the start of Timaeus' discourse. In this passage Timaeus refers to the colloquy that is to follow as μῦθος (likely story). We have already seen that the use of μῦθος in this context is very significant. It is in marked contrast to the frequent description of the Socratic enterprise in the dialogues as λόγος (reasonable discourse). Havelock suggests that the discourse of Timaeus is Homer/Hesiod myth-making. It is the "betrayal of the dialectic" (represented by the pursuit of λόγος or reasonable discourse). Since one possible way of understanding μῦθος is "fable" or "myth," the argument has decent textual support. Cornford also views the *Timaeus* account as mythic, but still believes that some Platonic doctrines and arguments can be mined from the mythic account.

Plato uses the word μῦθος (myth) very infrequently to refer to his own arguments (or tales).[41] For that reason, its usage here is highly significant. Socrates is usually taken by the non-Tejera/Straussian reader to represent the views of Plato in a dialogue. Timaeus, not Socrates, is the main speaker in this section. He describes his work as a μῦθος. Does this mean that his views are not those of Plato? If so, then the dialogue cannot be used as the key to unlocking Plato's psychological doctrines.

The significance of the usage of μῦθος is made even more intriguing by the vocabulary surrounding the story that proceeds that of Timaeus. Socrates, having recounted his image of the ideal state, expresses a desire to hear if it can be actualized. He says to his listeners:

> When I had completed my task, I in return imposed this other task upon you. You conferred together and agreed to entertain me to-day, as I had entertained you, with a feast of discourse (λόγων ξένια). Here am I in festive array, and no man can be more ready for the promised banquet.
>
> Hermocrates: And we too, Socrates, as Timaeus says, will not be wanting in enthusiasm; and there is no excuse for not complying with your request. As soon as we arrived yesterday at the guest-chamber of Critias, with whom we are staying, or rather on our way thither, we talked the matter over, and he told us an ancient tradition (λόγον ε'ισηγήσατο 'εκ παλαιᾶς 'ακοῆς)[42], which I wish, Critias, that you would repeat to Socrates, so that he may help us to judge whether it will satisfy his requirements or not.
>
> Critias: I will, if Timaeus, who is our other partner, approves.
>
> Timaeus: I quite approve.

Critias: Then listen, Socrates, to a tale (λόγου) which, though strange [ἀτόπου], is yet wholly [παντάπασι] true [ἀληθοῦς] . . .[43]

In this passage, Socrates requests a discourse from his compatriots. This is a common request on the part of Socrates.[44] For example, in *Gorgias* 527, Socrates says that he has given his friends a μῦθον (myth) and that, perhaps, as a result that they will despise his account. He cautions against this attitude. He prefers to believe the myth until a better account is given by his interlocutors. Hermocrates believes that Critias and Timaeus can comply with the Socratic request. This will be the feast for Socrates. Critias replies by giving a discourse that, though it is strange and ancient, is "wholly true." Gregory Vlastos points out that this same term, ἀτόπου (strange), is used to describe Socrates in the dialogues.[45] Far from casting doubt on the dialogue, therefore, the description "strange" ties it closely to the Socratic point of view.

Timaeus, on the other hand, presents only a probable myth. He lets down the side. This is the picture presented by the strong and weak-myth interpreter. While Cornford concedes that Platonic doctrines are found in *Timaeus*, Havelock, with the buttressing arguments about the dubious background of Timaeus himself, uses this to dismiss the entire dialogue as a regression unworthy of Plato.

Of course, just because the term is used in this section of the dialogue does not logically imply that it applies to the whole account. I have pointed out earlier that Aristotle and other ancients did not read the *Timaeus* in this way. Μῦθος (myth or likely story) may not be used in any technical sense here, whatsoever. I do not believe that even if μῦθος is applied to the whole dialogue, as both Havelock and Cornford do, that one can dismiss the dialogue as a mature reflection of the Platonic point of view.

The Havelock use of the term μῦθος (myth or likely story) as a pejorative is entirely unwarranted. The Atlantis account just finished by Critias has been described in this section as λόγος (argument or discourse). One is hard-pressed to find a story more mythic or fabulous in the traditional English sense of the term "myth" than that told by the ancient Egyptian priest to Solon.[46] Yet this account is consistently referred to by all the parties in the dialogue as a λόγος (reasonable discourse).[47] Additionally , not all stories told by Plato which are fantastic in nature are referred to by the technical term μῦθος. Why would the account of the rise and fall of Atlantis not be mythic, in the Platonic sense, while the story of the creation of the cosmos is?

Timaeus himself gives the answer at 29d in the dialogue. The account of the cosmos is an account about the world of Becoming. Exact and self-consistent knowledge about such a world is not possible. The best that Timaeus can do is supply a likely story about the coming into being of the cosmos. Such is the nature of any project that deals with the world of Becoming. This can, therefore, be taken as the best opinion that Plato thought he could advance about this uncertain topic. But why is the account of Critias, which also takes as its topic some facts about the world of Becoming, not also a μῦθος?

The motivation behind the account of Critias is to demonstrate that the ideal city described by Socrates that day obtained in the world of Becoming. Critias' description is an account that will allow comparison of the ideal city of Socrates with an actual city. This actual city is in the world of Becoming and hence unknowable in the robust, Platonic sense of knowing. But the purpose in the λόγος (reasoned discourse) of Critias is not to study ancient Athens in the world of Becoming, but to compare it to an ideal city of the world of Being. Since the city of Socrates can be known, the shadow city of ancient Athens and of Atlantis in the visible world can be studied. I will discuss this in greater depth when I turn directly to the text of *Timaeus*.

On the other hand, Socrates has not provided a full picture of the entire cosmos. Timaeus' project is, therefore, much more difficult than building a city in the shadow world. Critias begins with a basis of knowledge gained from Socrates' account of the ideal city on which to construct the shadows of the world of Becoming. Timaeus, who must picture the whole cosmic order, has no such full account from which to start. One is reminded of Timaeus' constant recourse to the ability to recollect the Forms in his description of the creation and existence of the shadows of becoming. There is even some textual support for thinking that Timaeus thought some appearances more nearly knowable than others based on their being like what the person with real knowledge knows about the Forms.[48]

Timaeus is careful to begin with the Forms. He begins his account with the things that can be known and tries to deduce his likely story from those things. The greatest difficulty is the great size of the cosmos. No one city can compare. Reason and discourse has produced a fairly full knowledge of the ideal city, but only fragments of knowledge and truth have been gathered about the entire cosmic order. For Timaeus to give better than a "likely story" about the origins of the world of Becoming in which humankind lives, he would have to have a full and complete account of the World of Being, the world of the eternal Forms. Such full knowledge, indeed such omniscience, would be possible only for a god.

This, however, destroys the case of the strong-myth commentator. Plato is giving the best account that he can give. These are the views of Plato. Better views would require a full knowledge about the World of Being.[49] Such a full account about the Forms could not be achieved in one lifetime. Common opinion holds that this is one of the capstone dialogues of Plato's career. He has learned nearly all he can about the World of Being, the world of the Forms, and with this lifetime of knowledge in hand he attempts to give his most likely account of the order of the world of Becoming.

This view of the use of the term "myth" in this context allows the weak-myth commentator to mine the *Timaeus* with confidence, at least in some areas, for advanced treatment of certain key Platonic doctrines. Some parts of the dialogue are not mere likely stories, but the fullest explications of Platonic doctrines that are given in the corpus. How does one separate these explications from other details that are perhaps more dubious?

The key to understanding which views Plato could hold with confidence is knowing which topics Plato feels have been most fully held up to the penetrating examination of the dialectic. Just as even the fabulous story of Critias could be used as λόγος in the context of the full account of the ideal state found in *Republic* (and summarized in *Timaeus*), so too could those parts of the cosmos be confidently described whose ideal types had been examined elsewhere. Knowledge of the Form of an object allows for a more certain account of the object.

It is also the case that Plato believes that some objects in the world of Becoming are closer to the World of Being than other objects. One can never have sure knowledge of any object that exists in the world of Becoming, but some objects are so "nearly eternal" and so "nearly changeless" that they can be the object of very strong, even likely opinion. The astronomical objects have already been mentioned as one case of this sort. What other sort of things would be Form-like enough to merit such increased confidence? It seems clear that the soul would be the best candidate.

The soul has been fully examined in several dialogues. Almost all commentators feel these were written prior to the *Timaeus*. To mention four prominent dialogues: the *Phaedo, Phaedrus, Meno,* and *Republic* all give extensive time to a λόγος (account) concerning the human soul. Unlike many of the other topics on which Timaeus must set forth a "likely story" regarding genesis and composition, the soul is the object of some knowledge.

However, it is worth noting that Plato is never sanguine about the chances of humans acquiring knowledge regarding the soul in any of his dialogues. In the *Republic,* the soul of the just and unjust human are believed hard to see and so an analogy with a city is created to aid in the sight of the soul.[50] Arguments are advanced regarding the nature of the soul, but Book X of the *Republic* still concludes with a mythic account of the soul's progress after death. Humans, as beings that exist in the world of Becoming, cannot be too confident of any putative knowledge of any of the things, even immortal souls, that are a part of that transitory world. Still, souls are not natural parts of that world, according to the Er account, and so knowledge about them may be more precise than is usually the case. The *Phaedrus* uses the image of the chariot to help the reader see what is being said about the soul in that dialogue. Souls are trapped in bodies. However, they are not bodies. Their motion and location make them hard to grasp. Their eternality and circular motion, which is the most regular of motions, makes them easier to see.

Compared to the cosmology of Timaeus in other areas, one would expect the description of the soul's genesis, function, and composition to be unusually complete and useful. In fact, one might speculate that if Timaeus had limited his discourse to the human soul, only then he might have been able to describe it as a λόγος (rational account).

Of course, Timaeus does not limit his discourse. He ventures into areas where the Form has not been so keenly grasped. He is mindful that even the account found in other dialogues enriched by this more complete explication of lineage and composition could not hope to give a full and perfect account of the human soul, obscured as it is by the confusions of matter. The account of the soul will, therefore, be mythic in the context of the cosmology. It will be, however, as close to a rational account as Plato can come when describing an object in the world of Becoming.[51]

The weak-mythologizer may, therefore, be correct in what she suggests. The *Timaeus* may be, at heart, a myth. This is to use the term μῦθος in a technical way. On this view, *Timaeus* is Plato's best account of what is an unknowable topic. However, given the unique nature of the soul, it may have a special status. It is left to Timaeus to picture this soul in the world of Becoming. Even with all the previous discourse, the vision will not be a sure one. At the end of the dialogue, the image of the soul presented will be as certain and as complete as Plato/Timaeus can make it. Therefore, *Timaeus* is the most full and mature working out of the vision of the soul available to the modern reader. Aristotle treats the dialogue exactly as if this were the case. The account of the soul is sure even if the whole is viewed as a myth, as Cornford uses the term.

Finally, both Havelock and Cornford ask questions about the style of the work. The *Timaeus* has many features that remind the reader of the works of Hesiod and Homer. Could such work be the thought of the mature Plato? Plato is critical of the reasoning and style of both authors in many dialogues.

The sister book of the *Timaeus*, the *Republic*, once again affords the reader an explanation of why Plato might have wanted to use this literary form. Plato in the *Republic* is critical of the writings of Homer in particular.[52] He views them as unworthy of the ideal human or state. They are full of bad examples and are written so that an imitation of evil is required on the part of the storyteller.[53]

However, Plato does not reject storytelling and myth as genre. He argues that the ideal city will contain only good poetry, not that it will contain no poetry.[54] In fact, at the end of the   *Republic* he tells a new and purified myth, the myth of Er. He also uses a false story about human genesis during the course of the argument of the *Republic*.[55] At 377c in the *Republic*, Socrates says that the ideal state will encourage poets to tell a good myth. Contrary to the fears of some commentators then, the style of the *Timaeus* is not a problem. It might be viewed as Plato's longest and most sustained substitute for Hesiod and Homer. Human beings need stories and accounts to explain their origins. Even a false story can be used to convey a truth. Plato provides his readers with a world-view, a mythic account, in the *Timaeus*.

There is no reason to believe that the style of the *Timaeus* gives the reader any grounds for dismissing the opinions found in it. Plato has commented on the need for good arts in the ideal state. Even if the dialogue is done for the purpose of providing this good art, that would not provide any reason to reject the contents of the dialogue. Good poetry for Plato would be the truest possible poetry. If *Timaeus* is a Hesiod-like account, then it is as true an account as Plato can make it. Good poetry or art for Plato is exactly that art which is accurate in its reflection of the Forms.

The *Timaeus* is the fulfillment of the promises of the middle books of the *Republic*. The two seminal writers of Plato's day told a cosmological tale and the story of a great military engagement. Plato has given us a purified Hesiod in *Timaeus* and in the *Critias* would have given us a glorified Homer. Could a better Hesiod contain many of the "noble lies" that Plato used to such good effect in the *Republic*? The reader cannot help but recall the invented story of the three races of humans composed of three metals. How does a commentator know that the psychological picture of the *Timaeus* is not just such a lie?

The answer is a simple one. Psychology is not the sort of thing that Plato would tell lies about to himself or his students. The "lie" about the golden race, for example, dealt with an issue that for Plato was not knowable even in theory. The origin of the human body or the development of any particular city were both fatally mixed with the cloudiness of the world of Becoming. As opposed to the human body or the body and soul composite, the soul in itself has special characteristics. Plato may not have always had all the information he would have liked to have had about the Forms or human souls, but both were topics that always received his most careful and profound attention. Plato did not care about details of the world of Becoming in the *Republic* except as they impacted on the behavior of his citizens. He felt free, therefore, to invent any useful story to describe body origins.

Plato wanted to create good citizens. To create a good citizen, however, it was necessary to know the nature of the human soul. That was a vital issue and one which required the keenest possible vision. Plato would not have obscured his sight or disabled his project by developing a "lie" in this critical area. It was one thing to have the populous believe myths about themselves in order to encourage good behavior. It would be another thing indeed for the philosopher to delude himself and his students with such lies. Just as the philosopher-king and the philosophers of the city knew the truth about their origins and mating customs, so Plato would have made sure that his own views and those of his students were as near to the truth as he could make them about this issue. Therefore, we might anticipate a sort of carelessness in the details regarding respiration, where any story would do. Plato would not have been so careless when it comes to the soul.

A.E. Taylor

In dealing with the *Timaeus*, I have found no single work more important than that of A.E. Taylor. His *Commentary on Plato's Timaeus* is easily the most thorough examination of the dialogue. At the same time, while it is illuminating on many key points, I believe Taylor to be almost wholly mistaken in his conclusions about the purpose of the dialogue. His hermeneutic goes awry despite his many keen insights. Taylor is a strong-myth commentator with an unusual twist. He believes, like the Straussian school, that it is difficult to discern the voice of Plato in any given dialogue. He goes even further than the Tejera-Straussian school by arguing that he has evidence that the voice of Timaeus is definitely not that of Plato.

It is Taylor's belief that Timaeus represents a sort of composite fifth-century scientist. Timaeus is a fusion of Pythagoras and Empedocles and so represented for Taylor's Plato the best that the science of the preceding generation had to offer. "It does not follow that any theory propounded by Timaeus would have been accepted by Plato as it now stands."[56] While Taylor does believe that he can, perhaps, hear the voice of Plato in the background of a particular passage,[57] he does not believe that most details of the theories found in those passages can be attributed to Plato. Plato has placed his dialogues in a particular Socratic historical setting and so is bound by the theorizing and conventions of the time of Socrates. Plato, according to Taylor, rarely writes anachronistically. If Plato thought the best science that the historic Socrates could have heard at a feast was a combination of Empedocles' and the Pythagoreans' ideas, then this is the only material that Plato will work with to make his philosophic points.

What according to Taylor is Plato's point in the *Timaeus*? Taylor believes that the *Timaeus* is an experiment. Plato relates a cosmogony of the world of Becoming in the language of the Pre-Socratic cosmologists. It is, for Plato, the best (most likely) story that can be told using that language. Plato would not, however, have been committed to many of the details. It is not the point of the dialogue to present Platonism. Platonism may lurk beneath the surface, but Plato can only use the language and the conceptual framework of the early fifth-century philosophers. It is important to note that Taylor often feels that Plato is expressing his views, but only in the most tentative manner imaginable. For example, in commenting on section 69c7 of the *Timaeus,* which deals with the human soul, Taylor says, "Thus we find Timaeus teaching precisely the tripartite psychology of the *Republic.* The only differences are that each "part" of the ψυχή (soul) is provided with a local habitation in the body...." He then dismisses those who would see a development or contradiction between the teachings of the *Timaeus* and the teachings of the *Republic.* Taylor suggests that the entire general Platonic psychology in *Timaeus* is borrowed from the Pythagoreans. It is only an idea used by Plato to aid in doing other philosophic tasks. It is not something to which Plato would be strongly committed.[58]

Obviously, this would prevent using the *Timaeus* as a key to a unified Platonic psychology. First, Taylor argues that the *Timaeus* is a good dialogue for finding the theories of fifth-century Greek scientists. One cannot turn to it to find Plato's ideas. Only on certain rare occasions could the reader claim that the voice of Plato could be found in the dialogue. Taylor himself says,

> ... we are entitled to say that Plato thought the view which arose from the fusion of Pythagoras with Empedocles the most promising line in fifth-century science and the one most directly connected with his own developments. It does not follow that any theory propounded by Timaeus would have been accepted by Plato as it stands.[59]

Second, it would not allow the reader to derive Platonic doctrines from the dialogue with any degree of confidence in those places where the voice of Plato did seem to be bleeding through the Pythagorean/Empedoclean arguments. If the presumption is that the *Timaeus* speaks of a foreign cosmology, the details of which are of little interest to Plato, then to use the *Timaeus* as a corrective to other more clearly Platonic dialogues would be absurd. It would be a case of using the dubious to interpret the reputable.

While his argument is quite detailed and a point-by-point refutation of his case is beyond the scope of this work, it is possible to summarize the major arguments that Taylor makes to support his strong-myth case. First, he believes that there is great internal evidence that points to the Pythagorean and Empedoclean nature of the cosmology proposed by Timaeus. Second, he feels that the doctrines found in the *Timaeus* are not those called Platonic by Aristotle. Third, he believes that the apparent contradictions between the cosmology of this dialogue and other Platonic dialogues, which Aristotle does not comment on at all, should lead the reader to read the *Timaeus* as a non-Platonic cosmological experiment. If both the Timaeus and the more orthodox dialogues are to be viewed as Platonic, Taylor wonders why Aristotle did not point to the obvious contradictions between the two in advancing his case against Platonism.

The account of Timaeus does bear the marks of both an Empedoclean and Pythagorean cosmology. This is not a controversial fact within the literature on the *Timaeus*.[60] What should be made of such a fact, however? Should every doctrine found in the *Timaeus* be attributed to the Pythagoreans or the school of Empedocles, even when direct evidence regarding Pythagorean or Empedoclean views in an area is missing?

I believe that there are sufficient reasons to deny that the influence of "other" schools goes nearly as far as Taylor would have it go. First, it is obvious that one may be indebted to an earlier thinker for important concepts, in fact concepts basic to one's whole view, without being a slave to them. The normal assumption in a philosopher of Plato's stature would be to look for influences in the work of the writer without assuming some literal correspondence between the two. Even Taylor, as we saw earlier in regard to the Platonic psychology, would not want to make Timaeus a mere mouthpiece for the Pythagoreans or any other school. To do this would be to deny Plato the importance as a thinker that even his contemporaries assigned to him. Plato would become a sophisticated Xenophon, content to parrot the views of his teacher and the contemporary society. Empedocles and Pythagoras, with the schools that grew out of their works, provided some of the conceptual framework for the *Timaeus*. This moderate vision of influence on Plato's work would not be adequate for Taylor's purposes, however.

Having gained an intellectual framework from earlier writers, Plato then proceeded to move beyond it and even to contradict it in many ways. What makes this more moderate view of influences on the formation of the *Timaeus* credible? To cite one example: the concept of a receptacle or space that could exist between that which is and that which is becoming would not be a concept that one would expect to find in fifth-century Pythagorean thinking. It is a novel and wholly unexpected development of the earlier Pythagorean arguments concerning existence.[61] The mathematics were not unknown to the members of the Academy at the time of Plato, but there is nothing Pythagorean about the concept.[62] It is anachronistic in the extreme to attribute such a view to these pre-Socratic philosophers. The idea would have been impossible to develop for the mathematicians at the historic time of the setting of the dialogue. Coming from mouth of an Empedoclean Timaeus, the notion of space is exactly what Taylor seems to believe is impossible: a deliberate use of anachronism on the part of Plato in a major area of the work.

The most that Taylor can claim in his defense is that Plato is placing a much more fully-developed Pythagorean/Empedoclean cosmology in the mouth of Timaeus. Doing this, however, would destroy much of the force of the Taylor arguments. Why would Plato feel bound by fifth-century science in some regards but not in other? If Plato did not fear development in a key concept such as space, there is no reason to suspect that he would fear other developments in small details.

Concepts in the dialogue are borrowed from the pre-Socratics in some of the small details. Taylor uses these small details to argue that where large concepts seem unique to the dialogue they must be part of the lost doctrines of Pythagoras or Empedocles. This is not possible for Taylor to do when the dialogue talks about space. Therefore, Taylor argues that Plato is allowing later work from these schools to intrude into the dialogue. But this is not the simplest answer available to Taylor. He could most simply reason that Plato uses accepted scientific "facts" to fill in the details of his original cosmogony. The big picture is supplied by Plato, since this is the part that he is interested in looking at, while just enough detail is borrowed from the conventional science of the day to give the whole plausibility.

It is important to note that even on the Taylor scheme the *Timaeus* combines the work of two pre-Socratic philosophers. If it was the intent of Plato merely to give the best fifth-century science possible without the dangers of anachronism, then why go to the trouble of combining two views that were not combined in the fifth century? In short, if the goal of the *Timaeus* is to present a cosmology contemporary to the setting of the conversation, as Taylor argues, why would Plato not merely provide the best actual fifth-century science? It is just as problematic, if it is a problem at all, to combine two schools that were distinct in the fifth century, as it is to introduce a new cosmogony developed from the clay of fifth-century science into what is, after all, a fictional account of a conversation. In either direction, Plato has produced a new thing. Why not simply assume that it is almost entirely new, given his stated distaste for pre-Socratic philosophers?

It might be argued that the two schools were combined to provide the best fifth-century science that was not anachronistic in terms of the concepts found within the science. We have already seen that this will not wash in terms of the notion of space. Another example is easily supplied. The notion of an active and imitative Demiurge, as opposed to the comparatively less active Mind of Anaxagoras is foreign to the fifth-century mind. It is a fourth-century concept, if it is not original to Plato himself. The whole Taylor notion that Plato must not be presenting a new cosmological theory because of the dramatic date of the dialogue is quickly brought to ruin.

Much of Taylor's handling of later problems in the dialogue are dealt with on the basis of the assumption that his Empedoclean/Pythagorean hypothesis is true. If a particular line of argument in the dialogue is not found in extant fragments from either school, Taylor assumes that the teaching must be part of the unknown writings of that school. We have seen in two key areas (the space and the Demiurge) that Plato seems to innovating. Must we assume that such notions are also borrowed from one of the two earlier schools? What will be left of Plato as an original thinker? In the psychology itself, Taylor sees a perfect harmony between the views of the *Timaeus* and the views of more orthodox Platonic dialogues. Why should he not view these as also being borrowed from either Empedocles or Pythagoras?[63] After all, the psychology is also an achronistic! To carry the Taylor argument to its logical conclusion would be to make key Platonic doctrines in the *Timaeus* those of the schools of Pythagoras or Empedocles. This attribution would have to be carried over to earlier Platonic dialogues, like the *Meno*, where no such pre-Socratic debt has been seen. Little would be left of Plato the original philosopher. Arguments from silence or from the scarcity of the textual record are dangerous arguments indeed.

Taylor has an immediate problem in pressing his general case. Just as Aristotle was the stumbling block for Tejera and Strauss, so

Aristotle makes Taylor's novel view about the dialogue much less plausible. As he points out himself, Aristotle frequently quotes the *Timaeus* as being the work of Plato. Taylor attempts to escape this problem saying,

> ... it is no evidence of the falsity of my proposed method of interpretation that Aristotle sometimes speaks of the statements of the dialogue as those of 'Plato.' This is, in any case, as natural as our own way of quoting the reflections of Hamlet as 'Shakespeare's.'[64]

This is surely an inadequate explanation, however, and is the only answer that Taylor gives for this serious problem.

Why do I view such a response as inadequate? First, as stated earlier, Aristotle is our best witness to the philosophic opinions of Plato. Taylor makes a strong case later in his commentary on the silence of Aristotle regarding a putative contradiction in the Platonic cosmology. By doing so, he concedes Aristotle's general value as a commentator on Plato's views. Any supposed evolution of the Platonic cosmology, which would have taken place during a time when Aristotle was at the Academy, occurs in an area where Aristotle is at great pains to refute any commentator who disagrees with him. This area deals with the attribution of motion to the Earth. The *Timaeus* seems to give some mysterious movement to the Earth. Taylor believes that if there is a contradiction between an early and late Platonic view in this area that Aristotle would have pointed it out. Earlier dialogues seem to postulate a stationary earth; the *Timaeus* calls these ideas into question. If the *Timaeus* contains the arguments of Plato, then, acccording to Taylor, Aristotle should have pointed out this problem.

The difficulty with this line of reasoning is that it is not clear what Plato thought about this issue. Ancient commentators do not agree on this very question.[65] It is not implausible to believe that Aristotle would have misinterpreted the thrust of an individual Platonic argument, particularly in an area where his own inclinations would have led him to a different conclusion. Everyone agrees that the text in *Timaeus* is unclear on the motion or lack of motion for the Earth. Ancient commentators disagreed on this score. This would have allowed Aristotle to select from a number of possible readings of the late Platonic doctrine on the movement of the Earth. It is clear that the early Plato believed that the Earth did not move. Charity to his master would have led Aristotle to see passages in the *Timaeus* that seemed to contradict both his own and Plato's earlier views on the Earth's motion in their most favorable light. In any case, it is not difficult to believe that years after hearing a particular Platonic doctrine, even Aristotle might have misunderstood it.

On the other hand, it is hard to believe that Aristotle would not have alerted his reader to the unusual status of the ideas in *Timaeus*. If Taylor's thesis is correct, then Aristotle had a guidebook to fifth-century science, but used it as if he were dealing with the views of Plato. Aristotle quoted from the dialogue many times.[66] He had ample opportunity to clarify the situation. We might write of the reflections of Shakespeare when talking about Hamlet's thinking, but we would not attribute the views of Hamlet to Shakespeare without a great deal of preliminary argument. This is exactly what Taylor, however, claims that Aristotle can do. This does not seem nearly as plausible as simply stating that in one area Aristotle made the most charitable reading of his mentor the favored one.

Finally, let me repeat that it does not harm my case to concede that some elements of the *Timaeus,* some less important details, may be borrowed straight from pre-Socratic philosophers. The question of the Earth's movement is far from central to the issues raised in the *Timaeus*. There is no reason to doubt that many of the details about motion might have come from the congenial school of the Pythagoreans. In borrowing such smaller ideas, Plato may have introduced contradiction into his own notions about the world of Becoming. Given his own hesitancy about the possibility of a coherent view regarding this world, such a contradiction might not have disturbed him greatly. Notions about the motion of the Earth did not occupy a central place in the problems and solutions of the dialogues.

Taylor, therefore, has failed to sustain his argument. He has correctly pointed out important influences in the development of some of the science of the dialogue. He takes this evidence much further than other scientific developments in the dialogue will allow. His argument from Aristotle cuts both ways. His clinching argument in this area is at best an argument from the unknown intentions of Aristotle. Given the repeated attribution of the views of the *Timaeus* to Plato by Aristotle, it seems best to retain the traditional reading of the text. The *Timaeus* represents the views of Plato and not those of a non-existent fifth-century scientist.

Reading the *Timaeus*

How should the careful student of Plato read the *Timaeus*? It is not enough for me to argue that previous readings of the dialogue have been wrong. Let me briefly describe my own preferred method of reading this important dialogue. I will attempt to demonstrate that the *Timaeus* is the most complete and clear word on the nature of the soul. In other words, the *Timaeus* is not just an account by Plato of his psychology, but the key account.

First, my discussion will not depend on whether the *Timaeus* is either a late Middle or a late dialogue in terms of the date of its composition. Regardless of the dating of the *Timaeus*, a critic of my thesis would have to further demonstrate the validity of certain hermeneutical and biographical ideas held apart from her or his ideas about the chronology of the dialogues.

From the seminal work of both G.E.L. Owen and his chief critic, H.F. Cherniss,[67] it is clear that one motivation of those who wish to move the dialogue from the later period, where it had historically rested, to the earlier period is to remove the explicit doctrinal statements of the dialogue from the mature period of Plato's thinking. Philosophers, like Owen, who wish to view the mature Plato through the lens of the more critical dialogues, best exemplified by the *Parmenides*, are uncomfortable with the dogmatic Plato of the *Timaeus*. In the debates over the place of the *Timaeus* in the chronology of the Platonic corpus, this only one that impacts my reading of text.

I believe that a late date for *Timaeus* is preferable, but that an earlier *Timaeus* is not by any means fatal to my thesis. An early cosmology would only damage my general argument if other, highly debatable, notions could be demonstrated. For example, the inclination that a later *Timaeus* would be of greater significance in determining Plato's thought often rests on the intuition that one's final statement on a issue is the authoritative "last word."[68] Last reasoning is best reasoning. Especially amongst the ancient commentators, maturity in a philosopher was taken to bring with it added wisdom and insight. Proclus, for example, in Book One of his *Commentary on Plato's*

Parmenides assumes the youthful Socrates of the dialogue is more apt to err than the older Zeno. He warns the reader not to give the young Socrates the respect Socrates is due in his maturity.[69]

What of this notion? There is no logical connection between a thought being last and being best. Philosophers can become less adept or more adept with age. The image of the modern thinker who, as he grows more conservative with age, repudiates the interesting work of his youth is too familiar to need repetition here. Xenophon, at least, would seem to demonstrate that such a human was not unknown in the ancient world. Just as growing older does not always bring this rigidity of thinking, so it does not always confer the blessings of wisdom. One would have to demonstrate that Plato did in fact progress in order to advance the overly simple thesis that "later is better."

The more subtle commentators usually argue that last work at least gives the final thinking on the subject by the philosopher. This, for example, is the position of G.E.L. Owen. Some commentators see the later Plato going through a time of inner doubt as to the rationality of some of his earlier doctrines. If the *Timaeus* is a late dialogue, then these doubts were less than some have suggested. I have already argued that the *Timaeus* is Plato's opinion on ideas related to the soul. A late position for the dialogue would, therefore, destroy the notion that Plato rejected doctrinal teaching on the soul in his last years. If the dialogue is early, then Owen might be right in arguing that Plato had no unified view of psychology over the course of his career.

Traditionally, the *Timaeus* has been considered one of the last of Plato's works. It contains many passages restating the basic psychology of such works as the *Republic*. A late *Timaeus* would forbid, or at the very least make much more difficult, Owen's notion that Plato underwent a radical change of heart regarding his psychology. A late *Timaeus* is not necessary to a unified Platonic psychology, but it is helpful.

Owen's attack is not directed primarily at Plato's psychology, but at the theory of Form. For my purposes, Owen may be dismissed by making two points. First, many scholars in this area believe the *Timaeus* to be a late dialogue. If *Timaeus* is a late dialogue, then the notion of the soul is not one of the possible candidates for a Platonic "recantation." Second, that even if the *Timaeus* is assumed to be late middle, it does not follow that the later dialogues carry more Platonic authority in this area. This means that even if the Owen position on dating turns out to be correct, one need not accept the Owen position on Plato's putative philosophic evolution.

The first task is the easiest. Most of the commentators on Plato have viewed the dialogue as the product of Plato's maturity.[70] Cherniss points out that Plutarch, the first to date the work, also held this view. Regarding the *Timaeus* and *Critias* he says, "But he was late in the beginning, and ended his life before his work."[71] Contemporary philosophers who have argued for a late date have included such diverse philosophers as Cornford, Taylor, and Eric Havelock. Once again, I am not suggesting that this means that the late view is, therefore, shown to be valid. I am suggesting that the notion of a late *Timaeus*, which is at least congenial to my general argument, is very close to a philosophic orthodoxy in ancient and modern philosophical reflection on the topic.

It is not necessary to refute Owen's views on Plato's alleged philosophical evolution in any great detail. A philosopher may enrich his views without radically modifying or abandoning them. If Owen is right, and the *Timaeus* and the unfinished *Critias* are the crowning works of Plato's dogmatic middle years, then it does not follow that they would not contain his lasting opinions about the human soul. Why doesn't he mention these dogma, if he still believes them? The late dialogues that Owens accepts as late are not mainly concerned with psychology. I will argue in a later chapter that in those areas where they do briefly discuss the human soul that they are fully consistent with the *Timaeus* picture. Owen's position is that Plato came to repudiate earlier dogmatic positions later in his life. Philosophers in the Owen tradition take the hesitations about the theory of Forms in *Parmenides* as indicative of the state of mind of the elder Plato. Many of the older, traditional Platonic doctrines are unequivocally present in the undisputed final dialogue: the *Laws*. Details are most often not present. Does this indicate a backing away from those details of Platonic psychology or merely the different focus of the late dialogues?

It seems to me that the argument of Owen is one case where the Tejera or Strauss-style critic has something to add to the debate. I have argued that, in general, one can derive Platonic doctrines from the general tenor and tone of the dialogues. The evidence of the ancient commentators, general hermeneutical principles, and textual evidence are usually sufficient to establish the larger doctrines. Can anyone but a dogmatic Straussian seriously doubt that something like a theory of recollection was Plato's best solution to certain epistemological questions? With notions of Platonic evolution of doctrine, however, the theories will always be massively underdetermined by the evidence.

All the commentators agree that no clear evidence exists to place the date of most of the individual dialogues. Ancient commentators are by and large silent on this issue (The one clear exception here is the dating of the *Laws*. All the ancients agree that it was written at the end of Plato's life). Ancients generally fail to see any great evolution in Plato's thought. It is certainly odd, for example, that Aristotle would not comment on any retraction by Plato of the theory of Forms. This was a notion that Aristotle certainly would have seemed happy enough to be rid of by any means possible. The texts and the ancients are of no help in finding Platonic recantations.

Modern commentators have made reasonable assumptions about general categories (early, middle, and late) for the dialogues. For example, most philosophers have agreed that early Platonic dialogues contain more of the Socratic elements, late dialogues less. They have disagreed widely, however, on the placement of certain key individual dialogues. Textual analysis has been widely criticized and has failed to yield definitive results. In their seminal articles dealing with this topic, both Cherniss and Owen concede that these methods are open to severe criticism and have failed to resolve the dispute.

Without a clear chronology from which to work, I contend that the philosopher is left with insufficient evidence to demonstrate a Platonic evolution or recantation based on the dates of the dialogues. I believe that I can demonstrate consistency in Plato's psychology, something that if it exists can be found or not found using only the texts without reference to their dates. If Plato's view of the human soul is consistent throughout the dialogues, then in this area, at least, Plato's views have evolved and not been revised. Owen himself could accept such a limited consistency without damaging his general position. I believe that the Owen position is, therefore, little threat to my views regarding the Platonic psychology.

Why then do I believe that one should read the *Timaeus* not just as an account of the soul, but as the account of the soul, if I do not rely on the putative fact that the dialogue is the last extended word on the subject? I believe that the very nature of the Platonic soul means that the *Timaeus* is the only dialogue available that could fully describe the soul. It is, in my opinion, the very sort of dialogue one would expect from Plato if he wanted to give his readers the key to his psychology.

It is important at this point for me to stress that I do not believe that giving his students the key to his psychology is necessarily the main point of the dialogue. Plato has other projects that he wishes to develop in the dialogue, some more central to the overall thrust of his argument in the *Timaeus*. However, as part of his overall effort to tell a "likely story" regarding the nature of the physical cosmos, Plato takes on the necessary task of making his psychology clear.

From the other dialogues, one point cannot be disputed regarding Plato's view of the human soul. The soul is the point of contact between the World of Being and the world[72] of Becoming. The very nature of the evidence leads to this conclusion. All souls that a human can see are incarnate. One cannot see a soul without a body. They provide the motion for the living body. Yet the soul is, consistently, in every relevant dialogue, described as being the part of any human most like the Forms or the part most divine.[73] Even if Plato had no consistent psychology, these are surely two ideas that he held with total consistency in all of the dialogues other than the *Timaeus*.

Plato also consistently held that one could have certain knowledge only about the world of the Forms. One could not have knowledge per se about the physical world, only true opinions. Writing a dialogue on the physical world and writing on an idea would therefore be fairly different projects. Each project would have a different goal and a different methodology. What would one do then when it came time to study the human soul in its native state? One must both study the body and the soul itself. It would be necessary to talk about both the world of Becoming and the World of Being, since the soul dwells within the one and imitates the other. This, however, would lead to an odd sort of dialogue. It would be in some areas no more than a μῦθός describing the formation of and composition of the human body. On the other hand, this dialogue must also contain sublime truth about the role of the Forms and the "most divine" human soul. To see the soul would require two things: seeing what a soul was without a body, a task requiring great skill in recollection, and seeing a soul with a body.

This unusual dialogue would need to describe both immortal and mortal objects. The body that contains the soul is mortal and part of the world of Becoming. Yet the world of Becoming, about which humans seem to know the most, cannot be the subject of actual knowledge for a Platonist. As Timaeus sadly concludes, humans can only have a likely story about such a world. The soul of the human, which every dialogue agrees is most divine, brings the philosopher to a description of its relationship to the World of Being. Unfortunately, the World of Being, about which true knowledge is possible, has been forgotten by humans after the pain of childbirth. These checks to the knowledge of even the most careful philosopher are constants of the Platonic view of the human soul in every dialogue where the soul is discussed.

What is left to the philosopher in trying to tell of both the incarnate and the free soul? All that can be recalled from the time when the soul was free of the body are myths and legends. "Science" (ε'πιστήμη), the investigation of the physical world, runs the risk of blinding humankind to the knowledge of this first, true world, the world of the Forms. Socrates rejects investigation of the physical world for himself in *Phaedo* 96b for this very reason. The dilemma is great. In seeking to tell the one story, the philosopher may prevent himself from telling the other. How can the philosopher investigate both the World of Being and the world of Becoming at the same time? One is reminded of the Socratic paradox proposed at the end of the *Phaedrus*. To write is to betray philosophy.[74] Plato, however, is writing when he transmits this very argument to his audience. How could this be? Just as Plato felt that he had solved this literary problem presented in the *Phaedrus* through the use of the dialogue format, so too the *Timaeus* is his attempt to investigate the soul, which is an active player in two worlds.

I believe that in the *Phaedo* the reader sees Plato dealing with this problem for the first time in great detail. The existence and immortality of the human soul are central concerns of the dialogue. How can the philosopher learn about the soul when it shares in both Being and Becoming? Most philosophers agree that the *Phaedo* is either an early or an early middle Platonic dialogue.[75] The reader can, therefore, turn to it for some of Plato's earliest extended attempts to deal with this issue. The *Phaedo* investigates the question of the immortality of the human soul under the pressure of the impending death of Socrates. Human souls have forgotten the only true knowledge they might ever have possessed of the World of Being. Socrates attempts to reassure his grieving friends by demonstrating that his soul will survive the physical death of his body. He attempts to do this through four arguments.[76] The arguments, however, establish only the bare existence of the soul after death, if they establish even that. The person who is examining the soul wants to know how to prepare it for the life to come. What happens to the soul after death? Do the goods in this world profit in the World to come? Socrates begins to examine these questions. He does not try to answer these questions by formulating sound arguments as he has attempted to do in establishing the immortality of the soul.[77]

Socrates in the *Phaedo* can only give a mythic account of the True World that the human soul experiences after death.[78] Only the bare fact of immortality can be reached through careful examination and words. Any information beyond this is clouded and subject to distortion.[79] Socrates is sure that the soul is immortal, but he can only tell a story to describe what happens to the soul after death. He suffers from the same constraints in the *Republic*. For this reason, he once again resorts to myth in Book X of the *Republic* when he must describe the fate of the soul in the other World.

But what of the world of Becoming? What can we know of this world? *Phaedo* gives the readers arguments for the existence of an immortal soul, but it attempts no description at all of the fate of the soul in the realm of the living, the world of Becoming. In fact, Plato does not seem to think such an account is possible at the time he wrote *Phaedo*.

Plato has a low opinion of the work of the pre-Socratic cosmologists. At the same time, Plato needs a means to examine the soul in both worlds. Anaxagoras comes the closest to finding a way and at 96b in the *Phaedo,* Anaxagoras receives a damning compliment from Socrates for failing to follow through on his (Anaxagoras') new methodology. Ironically, the *Phaedo* does not make use of the new method either. The question and answer format, the famed Socratic method, cannot reveal much about the world the pre-Socratic philosophers were so eager to explore. The *Phaedo* does, however, give some direction in how such investigation might proceed.

I suggest that the criticism of Anaxagoras by Socrates provides the blue print for another dialogue: the *Timaeus*. This passage is so important to my understanding of the centrality of the *Timaeus* to the Platonic psychology that I will quote it in full. At one point in his story about scientific pursuits, Socrates says:

... I heard someone who had a book of Anaxagoras, as he said, out of which he read that mind (νοῦς) was the disposer and cause of all (διακοσμῶν τε καὶ πάντων αἴτιος), and I was quite delighted at the notion of this, which appeared admirable, and I said to myself: If mind is the disposer, mind will dispose all for the best, and put each particular in the best place; and I argued that if anyone desired to find out the cause of the generation or destruction or existence of anything, he must find out what state of being or suffering or doing was best for that thing, and therefore a man had only to consider the best for himself and others, and then he would also know the worse, for that the same science comprised both. And I rejoiced to think that I had found in Anaxagoras a teacher of the causes of existence such as I desired, and I imagined that he would tell me first whether the earth is flat or round; and then he would further explain the cause and the necessity of this, and would teach me the nature of the best and show that this was best; ... For I could not imagine that when he spoke of mind as the disposer of them, he would give any other account of their being as they are, except that this was best; and I thought when he had explained to me in detail the cause of each and the cause of all, he would go on to explain to me what was best for each and what was best for all. I had hopes which I would not have sold for much, and I seized the books and read them as fast as I could in my eagerness to know the better and the worse. What hopes I had formed, and how grievously was I disappointed! As I proceeded, I found my philosopher altogether forsaking mind or any other principle of order, but having recourse to air, and ether, and water, and other eccentricities.[80]

As David Gallop notes in his commentary on the *Phaedo*, this project was carried out, not in the *Phaedo,* where it was inappropriate given the pressing time constraints of Socrates' impending death, but later, in the *Timaeus.*[81]

What is this new way of examining the world of Becoming? If one assumes that the world of Becoming was created by Νοῦς (Intelligence) for a purpose, then one can reason about that world in terms of teleology. The data of the senses, which for Plato cannot be trusted, does not have to form the basis of this new science. One can use unaided reason to come to one's conclusions about what Intelligence (Νοῦς) would have created.

This, however, gives the *Timaeus* the key role in determining the Platonic psychology. It is the only dialogue in which this teleological method is developed in full. What area will receive the most benefit from this new means of looking at creation? Only the soul exists in both the world of Becoming and the World of Being. The soul can only be seen in the light of its relationship between the worlds of Being and Becoming. The *Timaeus* is the only dialogue to attempt to do this. Therefore, it must be the dialogue that expresses Plato's clearest vision of the structure, function, and purpose of the soul.

Humans, as Plato knows them, have bodies. In that sense, if in no other, it is proper to speak of human generation. Humans, as body-soul combinations, can have a genesis, even if the soul cannot. Critias proposes in *Timaeus* 27 that Timaeus undertake the description of the genesis of humanity. Timaeus is quite clear that he will use the method of teleology. At *Timaeus* 28, when he is introducing his project, he turns again and again to the search for the Αἴτιον (Cause) as providing the impetus and direction for his discourse. By asking what Intelligence wanted to do in creating soul and what the purpose of the soul was to be in the cosmos, while holding ever before himself the image of the eternal Forms, Timaeus is using the method that will give him the best hope for success. It is the new teleological method in action. Like all human reasoning, it cannot be a perfect story, only a likely myth. It is a story that combines the dramatic and pedagogical force of the myths of *Republic*, *Phaedrus*, *Phaedo*, and other dialogues with the rigor of the teleological method of argument.

One final set of objections might occur to the reader. How does this method check the likely stories that have been handed down to the philosopher by tradition and suggested to him by imagination? Why did Plato use this technique to such an extent in the *Timaeus* and not with his other myths?

The teleological method allows the philosopher to tell a story or traditional myth and then subject it to criticism. The philosopher can say to herself, "Is this story of a genisis consistent with what Νοῦς (Intelligence) would do?" In other words, not just any traditional or imagined account will do. Reason must act reasonably. Any act of genesis or destruction must, therefore, be in accordance with reason. The philosopher can ask what the purpose, end, or function of any putative act of Reason is. Since Reason will act in a predictable manner, these are questions that have answers. It may not be easy to find these answers, the philosopher must experiment carefully using "likely stories," but the answers are out there to found. The fact that it is Reason at work promises this.

Timaeus is able to further limit the possible directions myth can move in by making a logical move based on the division of the cosmos between Being and Becoming at the start of his discourse. Being, for Plato, is consistently seen as greater than Becoming. Reason will, therefore, act to model or imitate Being as much as possible in the genesis and destruction that comes to pass in the world of Becoming. The world of Becoming cannot, by its very nature, cannot become the eternal World of Being, but particular imitations can be more or less like that stable world. Timaeus must look for a world of Becoming that maximizes stability, order, and the divine attributes. The myth that is most likely will be the one that comes the closest to achieving this goal, since the philosopher can rest assured that Νοῦς (Intelligence) will act in this manner.

Why didn't Plato use this method in his other dialogues? First, it is not clear that he did not use this method in the construction of the myths of the other dialogues. These myths all had, by comparison with the dialogue-length myth of the *Timaeus*, limited scope and function within their particular dialogues. The myth of the *Timaeus*, on the other hand, is the entire dialogue. In most other cases, the myth serves as an ending persuasive capstone. These myths are the speculative vision following the more certain results of the dialectic. It is important to note that most of these myths differ in cosmological detail, but not in the principles that gird their construction. The hollow world of the *Phaedo* myth, the myth of Er in the *Republic*, and the story of Timaeus all differ, but they differ least in those areas where teleology would be able to have the greatest impact.

What happens to the soul after death? The general answer is much easier to grasp than the specific cosmological details that flesh out that answer. The general answer to this specific question in all the dialogues is: "The soul migrates and receives rewards and/or punishments based on its earthly sojourn." The myths agree. The details, what the "undiscovered country" is like, are not always the same. The teleological-mythic method gives the philosopher a cosmology that approaches truth better than that of the pre-Socratic philosophers, but the theories produced are always underdetermined by the evidence. In this sense, Plato may have been in advance of contemporary philosophy of science, which has only recently begun to recognize that all scientific theories have this underdetermined status.

One final speculation is in order. If the *Timaeus* is a late dialogue, perhaps it is Plato's most refined experiment in allowing his contemplations about Νοῦς (Intelligence) to shape his mythic vision. Certainly, most commentators agree with the chronological order of *Phaedo, Republic, Timaeus*. These dialogues show an increasing elaboration and sophistication in the myths presented. It is also important to note that the *Republic* myth is more like the *Timaeus* myth in detail than the *Phaedo* myth is like the *Timaeus* myth. Of course, I have already pointed out that theories about Platonic progress are easily led astray, because of the paucity of evidence regarding the time of composition for each of the dialogues. However, those philosophers who are tempted to see such progress in Plato might look for it in the increasing sophistication of the mythology Plato uses.

I believe that this demonstrates beyond a doubt that if Plato has a consistent and interesting account to give regarding the human soul that the critical place to find that account must be in *Timaeus*. Every other dialogue in the Platonic corpus simply fails to consider both the World of Being and the world of Becoming in a way that can hope to provide a clear vision of the human soul in its totality. Those dialogues that do take up issues regarding the soul do so by means of either pure hypothesis, using stories that may or may not be true, or by the dialectic to establish singular characteristics about the soul in order to establish some broader point. Only the *Timaeus* considers the soul in both its incarnate and its free forms. Only the *Timaeus* uses the search for a cause to act as check on the myths that have been given to the philosopher regarding the soul. The *Timaeus* is truly the key to unlocking the Platonic psychology.

---

[1] See, for example, the seminal work by Frederick Copleston,   *A History of Philosophy,* Vol. 1. "But it is difficult to believe that Plato ever worked out his psychology systematically...." Copleston, Frederick. *A History of Philosophy,* 9 vols. (Garden City, New York: Image Books, 1989), Vol. 1: *Greece and Rome,* 209.

[2] Leo Strauss   and A.E. Taylor   are two leading philosophers who have questioned whether Platonic opinions should be gathered from the *Timaeus.*

[3] The ancient commentator Proclus   certainly took this view. Contemporary philosophers such as T.M. Robinson, F.M. Cornford, and Gregory Vlastos have also taken this view. Robinson, T.M. *Plato's Psychology.* (Toronto: University of Toronto Press, 1970.) Cornford, F.M. *Plato's Cosmology.* (London:

Routledge and Kegan Paul), 1977. Vlastos, Gregory. "The Disorderly Motion in the *Timaeus*." In *Studies in Plato's Metaphysics*. Edited by R.E. Allen. (London: Routledge and Kegan Paul, 1965.)

[4] V. Tejera in *Plato's Dialogues One by One* gives a recent exposition of this view. Tejera, V. *Plato's Dialogues One By One: A Structural Approach* (New York: Irvington Publishers, 1984), 3-7.

[5] Leo Strauss articulates such a view in *The City and Man* . In chapter two he states, "Let us assume that the Platonic dialogues do not convey a teaching, but, being a monument to Socrates, present the Socratic way of life as a model." Strauss, Leo. *The City and Man*. (Chicago: University of Chicago Press, 1978), 51.

[6] Eric A. Havelock in *Preface to Plato* says that the myth of the *Timaeus* is "... the final betrayal of the dialectic...." Havelock, Eric A. *Preface to Plato*. (Cambridge, Mass.: Harvard University Press, 1963), 271.

[7] A.E. Taylor in his famous *Commentary on the Timaeus* is the chief exponent of this view. Taylor, A.E. *Commentary on the Timaeus*. (Oxford: Clarendon Press, 1928).

[8] In his "Preface to the *Timaeus*," Benjamin Jowett claims that Aristotle quoted the *Timaeus* more than any other Platonic dialogue. Benjamin Jowett, Timaeus *by Plato* (New York: Liberal Arts Press, 1949), xxiii.

[9] Vlastos , Gregory. "The Disorderly Motion in the *Timaeus*," in *Studies in Plato's Metaphysics*. Edited by R.E. Allen (London: Routledge and Kegan Paul, 1965).

[10] Tejera, 3-7. At times I will extrapolate from Tejera 's general principles to responses he and those who agree with him might make to my criticisms of his view.

[11] Tejera, 131.

[12] I take it that Leo Strauss would fit into this tradition, though not making exactly the same arguments. Leo Strauss, *Socrates and Aristophanes* (New York: Basic Books, 1966).

[13] Tejera, 4.

[14] This term is Tejera's and not my own.

[15] W.G. Runciman in "Plato's Parmenides " is an example of someone who places early Platonic views in the mouth of Socrates. He then has Parmenides refute those opinions. Runciman, W.G. "Plato's Parmenides" in *Studies in Plato's Metaphysics*. Edited by R.E. Allen (New York: Routledge and Kegan Paul, 1965), 150-151.

In the same volume, Gilbert Ryle effectively contrasts this view, or one like it, with the views of A.E. Taylor. Taylor views the dialogue as a Platonic joke. This seems to be a frequent move on the part of Taylor, as I will point out when dealing with his discussion of the *Timaeus*. Ryle, Gilbert. *Plato's Parmenides* (1939) in *Studies in Plato's Metaphysics*, edited by R.E. Allen (New York: Routledge and Kegan Paul, 1965), 97-100.

[16] Aristotle *Physics* 209b11.

[17] For example, the principle of charity would demand that, as a philosopher, we should "maximize the number of true sentences" held to be true by Plato. The reader would, of course, take into account the historical setting of Plato. (This common definition of the charity principle is drawn from the *Dictionary of Philosophy* (New York: St. Martin's Press, 1979), 84.

[18] He spends a whole chapter dealing with irony. In "Interdialogical Interlude I," he struggles to define irony.

[19] Tejera, 75.

[20] I refer chiefly to Aristotle, but also Proclus and other ancient commentators. None of them knew a distinction between Plato and his work.

[21] Havelock , Eric. *Preface to Plato* (Cambridge, Massachusetts: Harvard University Press, 1963), 271.

[22] Havelock conveniently overlooks the fact that the *Timaeus* was one of the few dialogues readily accessible to the scholar of the Middle Ages. When other texts became more widely available, they were translated into Latin and used.

[23] I will refer to them as strong-myth commentators.

[24] That is, Socrates is present in the dialogue. The situation is *not* parallel to the *Laws* where the Athenian speaks without Socrates being present and so can be viewed as a kind of Socrates-substitute.

[25] "Of Timaeus of Locri nothing authentic is known...." So says R.G. Bury in his introduction to Loeb's *Timaeus*. Cornford adds (in *Plato's Cosmology*), "There is no evidence for the historic existence of Timaeus of Locri."

[26] These arguments are neatly summarized in Gregory Vlastos ' article: *The Disorderly Motion in the Timaeus*.

[27] *Timaeus* 29d.

[28] Cornford, F.M. *Plato's Cosmology* (London: Routledge and Kegan Paul, 1977), 31.

[29] ibid.

[30] Robinson describes Plutarch's analysis as "literalist." (Robinson, 59.)

[31] I am not claiming that Parmenides is necessarily giving the views of Plato. I am also not claiming he does not. It is only important to my point that the *Timaeus* is not the only dialogue where Plato *may be* giving his point of view without using the mouth of a present Socrates.

[32] I mean the Platonic doctrines such as the Forms and recollection.

[33] One should of course be careful not to attribute all details of Aristotle 's interpretation of Plato to Plato. It is much easier to be confused about what one's teacher means, then about what one's teacher has actually said.

[34] *Timaeus* 28a.

[35] *Timaeus* 86e.

[36] I am of course assuming, contrary to A.E. Taylor , that the tradition that Timaeus was a Pythagorean thinker is questionable. Taylor says, "Plato does not mention that he was a Pythagorean, though no one has ever doubted the

tradition...." (Taylor, 17). Several commentators do doubt this tradition including Cornford, 3.
[37] Plato, *Laws*. Translated. by Thomas L. Pangle   (Chicago: University of Chicago Press, 1988), 377-379. On 379 Pangle writes, "In the *Laws* we learned what Socrates would have said...."
[38] Jowett B., *Republic* (World Library of the Future: Electronically Enhanced Text © Copyright 1991, 1992, World Library, Inc.), 530a.
[39] Cornford, 3.
[40] Plato, *Lesser Hippias*. Translated by B. Jowett in *The Collected Dialogues of Plato* edited by Edith Hamilton (Princeton: Princeton University Press, 1987) 206.
[41] In a footnote on page 75 of volume II of Paul Shorey's translation of the *Republic,* he quotes E. Frutiger, "Frutiger, *Les Mythes de Platon*, says 'Plato uses the word only once of his own myths, *Polit* 268e." I do not think this is correct, but it does indicate that Plato uses the word very sparingly about his own arguments.
[42] I prefer to translate this as "a story related by ancient tradition." Jowett   loses the force of the passage altogether.
[43] Plato, *Timaeus* 20e. Translated by B. Jowett (Electronically Enhanced Text © Copyright 1991, 1992, World Library, Inc.).
[44] See for example the charge of Socrates to Polemarchus in *Republic* 331e.
[45] Vlastos, Gregory. *Socrates: Ironist and Moral Philosopher* (Ithaca: Cornell University Press, 1991), 1.
[46] I recognize that a few readers have assumed that the   *Timaeus* account of Atlantis is sober history. Their position is neither tenable nor one given much credence by the broad community of scholars. I will make, therefore, no further comment on it.
[47] *Timaeus* 26e and numerous other places.
[48] *Timaeus* 51b-51c. See the comments by A.E. Taylor   on page 334 of his *Commentary* and the response by Cornford at 191 of *Plato's Cosmology*.
[49] Taylor hints at such a solution on 333 and following in his   *Commentary*. I follow Taylor on this point and not Cornford.
[50] *Republic* 368d.
[51] One is reminded of the "bastard" reasoning that Plato speaks of in the dialogue when discussing Space at 51e (Cornford translation, 192).
[52] *Republic* 392e for example.
[53] *Republic* 411a for example.
[54] *Republic* 412b.
[55] *Republic* 468e for the use of the concept of the "golden race" by Plato.
[56] Taylor, A.E. *Commentary on Plato's Timaeus* (Oxford: Clarendon Press, 1928), 19.
[57] Taylor, 130-131.
[58] Taylor, A.E. *Commentary on Plato's Timaeus* (Oxford: Clarendon Press,

1928), 496-500.

[59] Taylor, 19.

[60] See for example: Grote, George.   *Plato and the Other Companions of Socrates* (London: John Murray, 1867), 243-247.

[61] Taylor concedes this point on page 313 of his commentary: "If that is true, Timaeus would be in advance of many of his own order in his clear conception of a things so abstract as 'timeless space."

[62] ibid.

[63] In fact, Taylor   comes very close to doing this at several points. See, for example, his discussion of the soul on page 497.

[64] Taylor, 12.

[65] A point Taylor himself concedes on page 226 of his commentary.

[66] See for example:

> Aristotle, *Physics* 209b11.
> Aristotle, *Physics* 210a2.
> Aristotle, *On the Heavens* 306b20.
> Aristotle, *Metaphysics* 1019a4.

[67] See the two superb articles by Owen   and Cherniss   in   *Studies in Plato's Metaphysics* edited by R.E. Allen (New York: The Humanities Press, 1965), 313-378.

[68] Owen himself does not advance this argument. However, many persons supporting such a thesis have an implicit commitment to this intuition.

[69] Proclus, *Commentary on Plato's* Parmenides. Translated Glenn R. Morrow and John M. Dillon (Princeton: Princeton University Press, 1987), 92.

[70] Cherniss, H.F., 339.

[71] Plutarch, *Lives*. Translated by Bernadotte Perrin (Macmillan: Loeb Classical Library, 1914) XXXII, 3.

[72] I shall not capitalize the word "world" in referring to Becoming. This is to keep the distinction between the World that "is" and the world that "is becoming" clear.

[73] This is especially clear in the arguments for immortality in the   *Phaedo*. See for example:

> Cyclical argument at *Phaedo* 69e-72d.
> Recollection argument at *Phaedo* 72e-77d.
> Affinity Argument at *Phaedo* 77e-80b.
> Final argument at *Phaedo* 102b-106e.

[74] *Phaedrus* 278.

[75] David Bostock places the *Phaedo* as the first of the Middle Period dialogues; David Gallop agrees. On the other hand, G.M.A. Grube places the dialogue in the earliest group. Perhaps the best position is that of G.R. Ledger. Ledger did a computer analysis of the canon that placed *Phaedo* in the "early middle group." Bostock, David. *Plato's* Phaedo (Oxford: Clarendon Press, 1986), 2. Brandwood, L. "Stylometry and Chronology" in *The Cambridge Companion to*

Plato. (Cambridge: Cambridge University Press, 1992), 112. Gallop, David. *Plato,* Phaedo (Oxford: Clarendon Press, 1980), 74. Grube, G.M.A. *Plato's Thought* (Indianapolis: Hackett, 1980), xii.

[76] *Phaedo* 69e-80b and 102b-106e.

[77] *Phaedo* 107-115.

[78] *Phaedo* 107b-115b.

[79] See   *Phaedo* 107b-115b and the odd details about the world Socrates includes.

[80] *Phaedo* 97c-98b.

[81] Gallop, David. *Phaedo* (Oxford: Clarendon Press, 1980), 174-175.

CHAPTER 2: THE PSYCHOLOGY OF THE *TIMAEUS*

The Opening Platonic Moves

I have established that the psychology of the *Timaeus* should be taken as Plato's mature view. Furthermore, I have given good reason to believe that the *Timaeus* will be the key to understanding Plato's psychology. What then of the dialogue itself? What is the psychology presented in the *Timaeus*, which I claim is centerpiece for Plato's full picture of the soul? The next chapter will function as a commentary on and an elucidation of Plato's discussion of the soul in this pivotal dialogue. First, I will try to set up the purpose and general tone of text. Then I will examine every mention of the human soul in the text. I will try to create a unified account of the soul out of this raw data I have gathered from the dialogue. Finally, I will answer objections that might be raised to my account based on details of the *Timaeus* and general Platonic doctrines. Then, in the final chapter, I will show that my view is fruitful in solving certain problems found in Plato's psychology.

It is significant that the opening portions of the *Timaeus* (17a-19b) closely link the dialogue with the account given in the *Republic*. Socrates briefly summarizes the arguments given the previous day to those who are gathered together. It is interesting to note that the most persistent interlocutor of the *Republic*, Glaucon, is missing from the *Timaeus*. In fact, all the speakers of *Republic* are missing save Socrates himself. In the *Republic*, however, one is given the impression that the gathering of interested parties is larger than those who speak, so one need not make too much of this fact. I would, however, suggest that Plato is involved in a bit of deck-clearing. He desires to go in a different direction from that taken in the *Republic* and so needs a new cast of characters. Glaucon and Adeimantus have helped Socrates see the just soul using one means of seeing. Timaeus is introduced to perform a different task.

It is not important for my argument whether the conversation being summarized here is exactly that described in the *Republic*. Some commentators like F.M. Cornford deny that this conversation is a summary of the *Republic* at all.[1] It is enough for my purposes that most commentators view it as recapitulation of the *Republic* and that those, like Cornford, who do not, view it as *Republic*-like.[2]

What do I mean by this? All commentators, including Cornford, view this part of the *Timaeus* as a summary of views very much like those found in the early books of the *Republic*. Minimally, Socrates is engaged in a conversation that substantially covers the same ground as the very early books of the *Republic*. He then takes an entirely different turn in the *Timaeus* from that he has taken in the conversation of the later books of the *Republic*.

Critias opens the *Timaeus* with an opening sketch of the Atlantis story. His comments are not important to the psychology that Plato develops in the dialogue. Socrates then turns to Timaeus, who will present the heart of that day's discourse. Timaeus is to bring the discussion from "the origin of the cosmos ... down to man."[3] He will utilize the idea of soul from the start of his story to the very end. It is the central concept of his entire tale. In discussing humans, he naturally lays out his doctrine of the human soul as part of the great soul-system that holds the universe together.

Timaeus uses a great many religious notions in his cosmogony and description of the human soul. This is in contrast to the *Phaedo*, and most of the other dialogues which discuss the soul. They are much more chary in their use of theological language. I will have more to say on this use of religious language at a later point. It is important, however, for me to stress at this point that I do not think that use of teleology or religious language commits Plato to a theological notion of the universe in the Western or Thomistic sense. A.E. Taylor and other Plato scholars picture Plato as being fairly close to Jewish, Islamic, or Christian theism. While open to that possibility, I will avoid the threat of anachronism brought with such readings and stick to a more open-ended, less developed picture of Plato's theology.

Timaeus has, in my opinion, two tasks. First, he must describe the genesis of the soul using as his guide the teleological principle outlined in the *Phaedo*. Second, he must show Socrates the soul of the human in action. He will describe the soul and how it functions in both the World of Being and the world of Becoming. In my opinion, he delivers a story that takes both issues into account.

In order to describe the functioning of the human soul in both the World of Being and the world of Becoming, Timaeus tries to give a likely story, describing the genesis of the world of Becoming and its relationship with the World of Being. Many of the details of the dialogue describe the genesis or function of various parts of the world of Becoming. These are not important to the Platonic psychology and so I will pass over them in my commentary on the dialogue.

Timaeus begins his discussion using the teleological method. Adopting the typical Platonic distinction, he divides his topic into those things that "... τὶ τὸ ᾿ον ᾿αέι, γένεσιν δὲ ου᾿κ ε᾿χον, καὶ τί τὸ γιγνόμενον μὲν α᾿εί, ο᾿ν δὲ ου᾿δέποτε?"[4] I translate this as "... What is it that exists always, having no genesis? Also, what is it that, on the one hand, is always coming into being and on the other hand never is?" Having created this fundamental division for all things, he places the entire visible cosmos in the second group. The cosmos is the world of Becoming. It is visible and has a "genesis."

He assumes that the world of Becoming will be created using the pattern of the World of Being. This guarantees that it will be καλὸν ε᾿ξ α᾿νάγκης (good from necessity).[5] This is the teleological principle in operation. Timaeus assumes that the cosmos and the creator are good. He develops his account of the soul, and indeed of the whole cosmos, based on these assumptions.

At 29c, Timaeus interrupts his discourse and warns again that his account cannot be without error. Socrates accepts Timaeus' caveat that this can be, at best, a likely story in some of its parts. The unfolding cosmology provides a strong reason for knowing that this will be true. Timaeus will deal at times in his account with things that were created as images of the true Forms. These images can, therefore, possess, at best, probability.

This is an important point in understanding the account of the soul that Timaeus will unfold for the reader. It seems fair to speculate, as I did earlier, that those things that are most like the Forms, or the World of Being, will also be the easiest for Timaeus and the others to grasp truly. The soul, which Timaeus will argue is eternal and invisible, is clearly one of the elements of creation most like the World of Being. While it is not a Form, and so no true knowledge can be gained about it, the opinions formed by the philosopher regarding this part of the creation will be the most certain of all the opinions in the dialogue. I suggest that the further the reader moves in the dialogue from the imitative initial creation of the cosmos by the Father/Creator the less "likely" the story will become. In fact, the text will strongly bear this opinion out. *Timaeus* 29b and 29c says (in Bury's translation) that

> those (accounts) which deal with what is abiding and firm and discernible by the aid of thought will be abiding and unshakable; in so far as it is possible for statements to be irrefutable and invincible, they must no wise fall short thereof; whereas the accounts of that which is copied after the likeness of that Model, and is itself a likeness, will be analogous thereto and possess likelihood.

Furthermore, it is the latter portions of the dialogue which contain the cosmological, physical, and physiological speculation that are so disappointing to the modern reader.

Following a last bit of Socratic encouragement, Timaeus plunges into the heart of his task. He reaffirms the use of the teleological principle in determining what would be produced in the world by making a quasi-religious argument for it. God, and Plato uses the word Θεὸς (God) in this section, is ἀγαθὸς (good).[6] As a result of this fact, all His work must be "good and fair." This God, constrained by necessity, will create bodies.[7] A rational body, however, is better or more beautiful than an irrational body. God will, therefore, create rational bodies.

Plato believes that reason can only exist in a soul. In this manner, Plato has provided a purpose for God creating the cosmos as a living animal with body and soul. It is vital to notice that at this point in the dialogue, when dealing with the genesis of the soul, that Timaeus describes this portion of his speech as "λόγους" (words) that are at best "εἰκότας"[8] (probable). He makes this even more clear at 29c, when he refers to probable words. If there was any significance in his earlier use of the term "μῦθος" (myth), he has switched from that term at this point. This tends to confirm my hypothesis that the details regarding the nature of the soul in *Timaeus* have a different and more clear status for Plato than other bits of the dialogue. At the very least, if the use of λόγος (word or discourse) in this passage is seen as accidental and of no great significance, it indicates that "μῦθος" (story or myth) in the dialogue is used as a word for an account synonymous with λόγος (reasoned account).

Two central questions are raised by this brief account describing the reasons for the soul's creation. The first deals with the nature of the God who is doing the creating. Some commentators have suggested that Plato's demiurge is just a word picture or image used to help make the myth clear to the audience of his day with their theistic inclinations. Though I have reservations about Plato's commitment to the actual existence of such a being, I will refer to Plato's God in the terms used to describe Him in the text. His existence or non-existence is not relevant to my central concerns.[9]

It is, however, important to remember that Plato is not describing the creation of the universe in time. There is no moment before the cosmos came to be. Early Christian commentators often conflated their own notions of creation with those found in the *Timaeus*.[10] There are differences between this ancient Christian position and that supported by modern scholars like A.E. Taylor. They are, however, alike in one important regard. Both modern and ancients in this camp have argued that the Platonic story of creation is very much like the account found in Genesis. The cosmos came to be in the strong sense.

The consensus of more contemporary opinion on the dialogue seems to be that Plato is not telling such a story. As F.M. Cornford aptly points out, Plato is not saying that the universe "came to be," but that it is "continually in the process of change."[11] I tend to agree with Cornford on this point. It is not, however, critical to my account of the human soul. I will take Plato to mean that the cosmos and the soul are created in the "Cornfordian" sense of coming to be eternally in imitation of the Forms and not in the Judeo-Christian sense of coming to existence out of nothing.

The second problem that faces the reader is the ease with which Timaeus adopts a dualistic picture of the cosmos. He states that reason is impossible without the soul. Reason does, however, exist in the world of Becoming. How does he know this? Timaeus is attempting to follow reason in this very dialogue. Timaeus can be relatively sure, therefore, that reason exists. The phenomena of a visible world also exist and most be dealt with by a cosmologist. Timaeus has, therefore, to explain the place of reason in his visible cosmos. Reason seems to exist in both the eternal and the visible worlds. How can this be? Answering this question will drive a good deal of the early formation of the Platonic psychology.

Reason in the Soul: Historical and Philosophic Considerations

Where should reason be located in the visible world? Timaeus quickly places reason in "soul." (This is quite literal, the text refers to "νοῦν μεν ε'ν ψυχῇ" or "intelligence in the soul.")[12] Why does Timaeus, and by implication Plato, feel justified in immediately postulating the necessity of a soul to serve as the instrument of reason in the human?

First, I believe such a view to be entirely consistent with the evolutionary direction of the Greek view of the soul. The early Greek view of the soul was not very complex. Soul was not a unified thing in these early accounts and was limited to humans. For Homer and his contemporaries the soul seems to have been "a precondition for the continuation of life."[13] It did not initially even have great religious significance. The soul was at times the seat of emotions and cognition. It also "represented the body after death."[14] It had no apparent connection with the rest of the cosmos.

The pre-Socratic philosophers developed the notion of the soul in many of the directions that Plato would take later. Thales, along with most of the rest of the society of his day, seems to have believed that the soul was the motive force for the body. Without a soul, a human being would be unable to raise her or his arms.[15] Heraclitus connected his human soul to Λόγος (Word) and the cosmos.[16] The soul concept, which had been expanded by earlier thinkers to include all living things, was now made a universal principle for all things.

In discussing Taylor's reading of the *Timaeus*, I have already noted the strong resemblance of much of the account in *Timaeus* to Empedoclean and Pythagorean teachings of this period. The notion of an immortal soul, a soul that energized the workings of the visible world, and the idea of an afterlife for the human soul were all postulated in the era prior to Plato. Depending on how one takes Heraclitus, it is even possible that a cosmic soul containing divine Λόγος (word) had already been suggested. In arguing for the necessity of the soul in the rational cosmos, it is clear that Plato is agreeing with the mainstream philosophical traditions of the day.

I believe, however, that an analysis of the text provides for a deeper, internal reason for the soul being necessary to a reasonable cosmos. It is based on a difficulty already present at the core of Timaeus' account. From Aristotle's time to the present day, a major criticism of Plato's theory of Forms has been the inability to connect the World of Being with the world of Becoming. In previous dialogues,

Plato has fallen back on analogical language to describe the interaction of the world of Becoming with the Forms. He has spoken of imitation and used craft analogies to picture the interrelation. How did this connection actually work?

One can be sure that this is a problem that also troubled Plato. I believe that he sought to find the solution in the concept of a human soul. Almost everyone at the time conceded the existence of this thing called soul. Soul was at least arguably invisible like the Forms.[17] Everyone admitted that it existed within humans at the very least. What if one postulated a substance that was not quite fully Being, but not yet fully part of the world of Becoming? Could such a thing be done without breaking the laws of logic? If so, then Plato would have a substance that could, perhaps, flow from the Forms and yet connect to and impact the physical world.[18] It is my suggestion that in soul Plato thought he had the most likely candidate for such a median position. If one assumes for the moment that the criticisms of the *Parmenides* are fresh in his mind, then this idea grows even more plausible. For Plato, soul might be the way out of his dilemma of connecting Being to Becoming. I will have more to say about this picture as the *Timaeus* account unfolds.

At the moment, it is sufficient to note that Plato has already made an important move in that direction. Parmenides had written in his famous poem that only "the is" can possibly be. G.S. Kirk summarizes Parmenides as saying that the world "cannot come to be or perish, change or move, nor be subject to any imperfection."[19] For Plato, the problem was that the world revealed to his senses simply did not seem to fit this picture of the universe. How could one make sense of the data of the sense organs in the Parmenidean cosmology? It was easy to be dissatisfied with the answers Parmenides gave, but frustratingly difficult to refute his arguments.

Plato's move in *Timaeus* is an ingenious one. He agrees with Parmenides that everything that fully is cannot come to be or perish, change or move, nor be subject to any imperfection. This is the World of Being, the world of the Forms. On the other hand, there is a second world. This world never, as a whole, comes to be. It has, strictly speaking, no final genesis, because it is in a constant state of coming to be. To use Plato's language in this section of the dialogue, the material universe is a world in flux. Strictly speaking, it is not. One can have, therefore, no real knowledge about it. The account taken as a whole is likely story.[20]

One must be careful in looking at the details of the text in this regard. In speaking about the world of Becoming, Plato frequently lapses into the language of appearance. Modern humans know that the earth revolves around the sun. In everyday discourse, however, they frequently speak of the sun rising in the West. This is a perfectly appropriate day-to-day usage, as this is what the sun in fact appears to do to the naked eye. The modern human is using, in that particular case, the language of appearance.

In the same way, it would be difficult to write about the world of Becoming without using the language of appearance. Fire, air, water, and earth seem real to humankind. It would be nearly impossible to write a readable account, with the linguistic and logical apparatus of Plato's day, that did not speak about the world of Becoming as if it actually is. Plato will, in fact, use the language of appearance frequently in the dialogue. I will often imitate Plato in his use of the language of appearance.

It is important to remember, however, that fundamentally for Plato this world is a Becoming world that is a copy of the true world of Forms. As Plato puts it in 29b, "Again, if these premises be granted, it is wholly necessary that this Cosmos should be a Copy of something." Later he makes the identity of the model clear in a passage dealing with the epistemic certainty of the account, "... for as Being is to Becoming, so is Truth to Belief."[21]

Despite Parmenides' early epistemological concerns, it is possible to think and speak about the world of Becoming. This world is always about to be, it is sensible and parts of it lurk on the edges of true Being. One can, therefore, opine about what it would be like if only it could, against all reason and expectation, come into full Being. To use Platonic language again, the world is in "constant state of motion."[22] Like Sisyphus, it is always going somewhere, but never getting anywhere. The word Plato uses to describe this non-place is "ἄτακτος (disorderly)." This is not a positive attribute, but the absence of the order necessary to accomplish any positive good. It is possible to talk about this place only in a sort of negative, or apophatic, language.

In Timaeus' cosmology, it is to this disorderly place that Mind comes to bring what order it can to the universe. How can it bring any sort of order to what must, in the strongest and deepest sense, remain unknowable and disorderly? Soul becomes the great intermediary between Mind and the disorder. This relationship will produce a κόσμος (orderly cosmos). Soul will be eternal and unchanging and yet the source of the motion for the entire cosmos. Even more vital to humankind, soul will act as the vital life force and the source of reason for the human. It will provide humans with both the motion needed to live in the world of Becoming and the stability necessary for true knowledge. Plato has provided a mechanism for opining about the running brook and knowing the Good Itself. A great cosmic soul, of which the human soul is an image, will perform these tasks for the cosmic animal.

Implications of the Cosmic Soul for Human Psychology

Plato spends a great deal of time describing the origins and functions of the cosmic soul. It is not my purpose to provide a detailed account of that soul. These questions will have to be set aside so that I can focus on the human psychology presented in the dialogue. I will discuss the cosmic soul only in areas where it has implications for Plato's human psychology. To understand what Plato is saying about the human soul, it will be necessary to briefly examine what he says regarding the cosmic soul. Some vital distinctions regarding simplicity, Greek thinking about mixture, and psychic motion must be made.

The body of the cosmic animal, which contains cosmic soul, is formed by imposing on the space or plastic of the universe the geometric patterns of the four classic Greek elements (viz. fire, water, air, and earth).[23] This animal is "indissoluble by any agent other than Him who bound it together."[24] This cosmic animal is shaped like a sphere and contains everything in the world of Becoming within itself. It lacks nothing. As part of this world it must move, but it receives the most perfect motion, the motion that is the most stable since one never gets anywhere. The cosmic animal "spun … round uniformly in the same spot and within itself and made it move, revolving in a circle."[25] The Creator cannot make it totally stable, it is the world of Becoming after all, but he does remove the other six motions from it.[26] This creature is called a god. Into this best-possible body, God places the cosmic soul. The soul stretches throughout the body of the cosmic animal. It encases the spherical body, which for the first time is now called οὐρανὸν ἕνα μόνον (one sole and solitary heaven).[27] The soul is, therefore, working to provide the motion and the direction of that motion to the cosmic animal. It holds the whole creature together. Despite the order in which he has related the genesis of the cosmic animal, Timaeus is quick to caution the reader that the soul is first in order of creation. It is superior in every way to the body composed of the visible elements. The soul has, therefore, a genesis. This makes it possible for it to be in the world of Becoming. It is a becoming thing, part of the work of creation.

Once again it is important not to confuse this notion of genesis with a Western notion of creation out of nothing by an omnipotent creator. Nothing in the world of Becoming ever finally "is." It is always becoming. In this sense, the soul is always in the process of genesis. The difficulty, therefore, for Plato, is not in asking how such a soul could be part of a body, but how such a soul will be able to have some of the attributes of the World of Being. This brings the reader of *Timaeus* to one of the most difficult passages of the dialogue.

Plato argues, at 35 and following, that soul is composed of a "third form of being" midway between the "being which is indivisible" and the "being which is transient and divisible into bodies." Can we identify this with being midway between the World of Being and the world of Becoming? An immediate problem for such a reading would be Plato's attribution of being to the world of Becoming. On the other hand, what else could Plato mean in this passage?

F.M. Cornford follows Proclus in arguing that Plato is talking only about a certain sort of existence between the World of Being and the world of Becoming. Cornford points out that in *Sophist,* when Plato ascribes being or existence to this new world, he intends "simply what is meant by the word 'exists' in the statement 'The potential to move exists (partakes of existence).'"[28] The potential for motion clearly exists in a different sense than the Form of the Just. The very motion that produces genesis is not the motion of full existence. It is a motion that is driving toward existence, even if it never reaches the mark. It falls short of the goal, but full Being is that goal. Plato is not, therefore, being inconsistent in ascribing substance or being to this world soul. The new world is not one of existence, but of partaking in existence. This position seems the best description of Plato's goals in the passage.

Plato combines Existence, Sameness, and Difference to produce the cosmic soul. The soul has these three basic elements, but each element is composed of two different parts. He takes indivisible and divisible parts for each of the three elements and joins them together in a great "mixing bowl." The picture is like a human mixing wine before a feast. The soul is distributed in portions across the cosmos in a numeric sequence equivalent to a musical scale.

There is much in this description of the creation of the cosmic soul that is relevant to the human psychology that will follow. First, I would stress the intentional obscurity of the account. Timaeus is looking into matters of profound ambiguity. The details of this myth are not nearly as important as the general impressions that one is left with by the accumulation of those details. Second, there is an emphasis on the composite nature of the soul. Third, the soul is created of the elements that will allow it to be the seat of reason in the cosmos. These are, as Bury points out, the three great Forms of the *Sophist*.[29] The composition of the world soul from these three elements will allow the world soul to recognize and identify all things. Finally, the musical order in which the soul is distributed in the cosmos reminds the reader of the fact that the Creator is imposing order on the world of Becoming. Taylor points out that such an imposition is consistent with and reminiscent of the cosmology of the Pythagoreans.[30] He concedes, however, that even here the picture is not just a take on Pythagorean philosophy, but a development of it.

The significant point for the Platonic psychology is not, however, captured in any of these comments. I believe the important point is the internal tension present in the formation of the cosmic soul. The soul consists of three elements. Two of these elements are opposites: Same and Other. Being functions in a median position between the two of them. In an even more explosive mix, each element is a joining of divisible and indivisible units. These are not pieces that are easily put together and they have to be forced into such a position.[31] One could easily imagine a soul that is, therefore, in constant tension, but that is not the case.

These disparate elements have, according to the text, become one. Plato describes them as "πάλιν ὅλον" (one whole).[32] The energy and life of the soul can be thought of as springing from this union of that which should not be capable of such total unity. This is a fusion that produces a great deal of motion as well as the capacity to know. At the conclusion of this section, in fact, Plato firmly declares (34c) that failure to recognize this fact is a failure to recognize the truth.

The soul keeps the individual characteristics of the Forms that are the basis for its creation: Being, Same, and Other. These initial characteristics will give the soul the ability to reason. Failing to go beyond the initial composition of the soul will, however, lead to a failure in getting the point of this section of the dialogue. More important than the elements' initial diversity is their eventual, radical oneness. They are combined to form one soul. This unity is overlooked or underplayed by commentators such as Taylor and Cornford when they discuss this passage. The initial disunity of the soul elements in the mixing bowl only emphasizes the utter unity the soul comes to possess. At the end of the account, Plato wants to think of this created soul as one.

The Cosmic Soul and Simplicity

What does Plato mean when he describes the soul as one? There are several senses in which he might be using this word. The strongest notion of oneness is simplicity. Can such a soul, both one whole and composite, be simple or is Plato suggesting something less than this in the *Timaeus*? In other dialogues, like the *Phaedo*, one gets the picture of a soul that is not a composite. How does one square this notion with the account offered here? For example, in *Phaedo*, Plato says of the soul that is it is "pure, uniform, and divine."[33] Can the one and whole soul of *Timaueus* is be thought of as simple, one in this strong sense? I believe it can be. I will demonstrate in what sense the cosmic soul of *Timaeus* is simple.

What is usually meant by the philosophic notion of simplicity? I take it that philosophers, including Plato, have usually believed that such beings have no parts. In Platonic language, they are not composite. Hence:

> S: For all beings x it is possible that x is simple if and only if, x is a being and x is such that there is not some thing y such that y is part of x and y is not x.[34]

A simple being is, therefore, its only component. Please note that this lack of component parts is only one piece of the usual philosophic notion of simplicity. Plato, however, has here in *Timaeus* described a soul with at least six components. On first glance, Plato's cosmic soul cannot be simple.

I think, however, that one should differentiate between beings that are essentially simple and accidentally simple. The usual philosophic notion deals with beings, like the Judeo-Christian God, that are essentially simple. An essentially simple being has no parts, has never had any parts, and could never have had parts. Such eternal simplicity is not a requirement of definition S. It only demands that the being x have no parts at present. The idea of essential simplicity (ES) might, therefore, include the following:

> ES: For all beings x and times t it is possible that x is essentially simple if and only if, x is a being and x is such that there is not some possible thing y or possible time t such that y is part of x at t and y is not x at t.

It seems possible to conceive of a being that has, at present, no parts, but that was formed from parts in the past.[35] One can imagine a being formed from the utter fusion of at least two individual things. This fusion is so complete that one being is the result. A dissolution is no longer possible. One new being has utterly replaced the two original beings. How many component parts are there in this new being? The initial elements are simply no longer identifiable in the new creation, even if the new creation possesses some of the characteristics of the original components. This leads to the following characterization of accidental simplicity (AS):

> AS: For all beings x it is possible that x is accidentally simple if and only if at the present time t, x is a being and x is such that there is not some thing y at t such that y is part of x at t and y is not x at t.

This solution raises an immediate problem. In the passages following 36d, Plato describes the soul being divided into two sections: the motion of the Same and the motion of the Other. This text suggests two questions. First, if the soul is AS, then how can it possess these two parts? Second, if the soul is AS, then why have the original component parts remained Same and Other?

There is an additional difficulty. In addition to characteristic S, philosophers have also held that simplicity includes the notion that a simple thing has only one characteristic. Theologians, for example, have argued that a simple divinity can only have one attribute. Traditional god-talk, however, presents the theologian with a problem. Folk usually ascribe multiple attributes to God (e.g. holiness, justice, goodness). The usual method philosophers of religion use to escape this problem is to argue that all God's attributes are one. God's love is equivalent to God's justice.

Whether or not this theological position is coherent, it is not an argument that seems to be open to Plato. As many commentators have pointed out, Plato has postulated these three elements in the soul just because of their individual characteristics. He needs the characteristics of these elements of the Same, Different, and Being in order to allow the soul to reason. In section 37b and following, Plato develops an account of reasoning that depends on just such characterizations. The Creator divides the newly formed soul into two circles. To one circle he gives the motion of the Same and to the other circle he gives the motion the Different.

Each soul circle comes into contact with other phenomenon of the world of Becoming in the course of motion. Each recognizes either sameness or otherness and is able to report this information through the soul-system. The accumulation and comparison of such reports evidently leads to the ability to categorize and know the world around the soul. Most troubling of all to the consistency of Plato's theory, the two circles seem to have a division of labor: to the circle of the motion of the Same goes the task of recognizing the things that are the same and to the circle of the motion of the Different goes the task of recognizing the different.

To summarize then, the reader faces three difficult problems. The first two relate to the Platonic doctrine that the soul is simple. First, the cosmic soul seems to have at least two parts. Second, the cosmic soul has three separate characteristics. Both of these features are difficult to reconcile with the idea that the cosmic soul is simple. Finally, having created a unified cosmic soul, Plato divides that soul into two sections, each containing motions whose names correspond to two of the original components. Has Plato unified a soul only to divide it again?

I believe that these very difficult problems can be resolved. It is critical to begin with an examination of the exact language that Plato uses in discussing the formation of the soul. The soul is at 35b referred to as being shaped into one form. Bury translates the passage, "And He took the three of them (the Same, Other, Being) and blent them all together into one form." This mixing is forced and unnatural. The image created by the vocabulary used (forms of μίγνυμι) is one of two armies forced together in the clash of a battle. The image does not, however, detract from the essential unity of the combination. The vocabulary used by Plato here stresses the power and potential of the combination. Plato describes the world soul as being first three and then in turn one whole.[36] It is difficult to imagine stronger language being used to describe the new state of the cosmic soul. It is one, no longer three. Each of the portions of the soul are composed of this fusion.

The Cosmic Soul: Simplicity and Mixture

If this were the entire textual account of the soul, the soul would qualify as AS simple. It is now one form.[37] There is a problem, however. Bury translates the next section as saying, "... and each portion (of the soul) was a mixture of the Same, of the Other, and of

Being."[38] Plato has, therefore, referred to the soul as both "one form" and a "mixture." On the face of it, this presents an interpretive problem. If by "mixture" Plato means what is produced when mixing items that are potentially separable, then the soul cannot in any manner be thought of as simple. It also makes it difficult to understand what he means by describing the soul as "one form." A closer examination of the language of the passage reveals what Plato meant.

The word translated "mixture" in passage 35b (μεμιγμένην) comes from the Greek verb "μίγημι." Μίγημι can be used to describe the mixture of two liquids to form a third. We are reminded by this word of the image of the wine mixing bowl found earlier in the creation account. It would appear from Aristotle's discussions related to "mixing" (or combination) that the pre-Socratic philosophers did not have a very sophisticated mechanism for dealing with the notion of combination or mixing. Aristotle says of them, "Nor did they give any account of combination . . ."[39] Aristotle suggests in this passage that prior philosophers have been content with popular notions. One example is the belief that mixing liquids produced a new substance. Aristotle, of course, repudiates this view, but it is sensible to attribute it to the less scientifically innovative Plato.[40]

Two wines can, on this simple view, be poured into a mixing bowl and a third wine be formed as a result of the mixing. The new wine has many of the attributes of the old one, but the two original wines can no longer be derived from the mixture. Each drop of the new wine contains some of the characteristics of both of the old wines that were used to form it. Each drop is a mixture, but each drop is one. The two wines have combined to form a new unity.

I would suggest that "mixture" here, therefore, refers to a union that is not dissolvable. Depending on whether the creation of the world is actual or only allegorical for Plato, this union may or may not have happened in time. In any case, the soul is in a "mixture" that is not dissolvable. The use of the term "mixture" on Plato's part is an unfortunate one. It is due to a primitive understanding of physics. Plato, given a modern scientific understanding of the laws of physics, could have used the term "fusion" as opposed to "mixing" to convey his meaning with greater precision. This would allow for his conception of the soul as being formed from original components that now have achieved the radical unity of being one form.

The Problem of Motion in the Simple Soul

Plato's primitive notion of "mixing" does not resolve the most serious problems in understanding the text. What about the motions he attributes to the soul? In the account, Plato divides the cosmic soul into seven sub-divisions.[41] These seven unequal circles provide the motive force for the seven astral bodies. Each of the five known planets (Mercury, Venus, Mars, Saturn, and Jupiter) receives its own track. The sun and the moon (viewed as planets by Plato) each has its own motion provided to it by a particular segment of the cosmic soul. In this manner, Plato provided a cosmological basis for the motions of the seven planets. He also tried to give a means that would later explain the retrograde motion of certain planets like Venus. He did this by providing each planet with its own motion. Speeds are also assigned to each planet. A combination of these two things provides a first step in explaining the observations of ancient astronomers regarding the motions of these bodies.

These astronomical gains, however, create problems for Plato's psychology. Things with parts cannot be simple. Plato argued in the *Phaedo* that things that are not simple must perish. Simple things are more excellent than compound things, and yet the "most excellent"[42] cosmic soul is apparently divided into parts.

In interpreting this early passage, it must be recalled that by 35b in his discussion of the creation of the soul, Plato refers to the cosmic soul as one whole. Plato is creating unities out of disparate elements. One of these unities is the cosmic soul and another is the total heaven. At 34b Plato refers to his complete cosmic animal, right after his discussion of the work of the cosmic soul as one. What does this usage entail? It is not a reference to the fact that there is only one universe. He uses the word solitary to make that clear. What is the implication of the one?

Plato must believe that the cosmic animal can begin with many parts and still achieve essential unity. In like manner, I will suggest a means whereby he can have the soul perform many functions in relation to the cosmic animal without compromising its accidental simplicity and radical unity in terms of its own being. This distinction is vital to my discussion. Plato felt that in the unique world between Being and non-being, he could create a unity out of many parts. The reasons for this confidence will be made clear at a later point.

This overview of the creation of the soul at 34b provides the guiding principles by which the rest of the section should be read. I view the discussion at 35b and 36b of the division into portions as providing a Form to the unified soul. What do I mean by Form? A thing can be simple, but still have a certain defining characteristic that separates it from other simple objects. I would argue that the geometric idea of line is simple.[43] Line qua line has no parts. One can divide the line into segments or pick out discrete points on the line, if one is so inclined, but the line itself has no segments or points as a part of its nature. A line, however, is not just a squiggle. There is a certain characteristic, straightness, that it possesses perfectly that marks it off from other ideas.

The division and portioning of 35b and 36b are Plato's way of describing the soul's defining characteristic. It is not enough to say that soul is that which is self-moved, its single attribute as a simple being. This definition does not show the reader how self-movement will function in the world of Becoming. The purpose, after all, of the *Timaeus* is not merely to define what a soul is, but to show its cosmological place. How will the visible react to this self-moved Form? This can be described, in common usage, as the organization of the soul within the cosmic animal.

It is important to keep in mind that the radically unified soul is simple in its pure form. The passages around 34b suggest that this self-moving substance expresses itself in different manners when placed in conjunction with different bits of matter and locations. The material universe comes into a set of relationships with soul that produces different directions in motion. Later Plato will suggest that the human soul can be confused in its motions by coming into contact with matter. How can the soul be simple and have these different motions and confusions?

The answer to this question is found in examining exactly what it is that Plato needs to be simple and hence immortal. Plato is not committed to the necessary immortality of any relationship of soul with matter. As I have shown, even the cosmos is only accidentally immortal.[44] God could destroy this most fundamental relationship of soul and matter. It is soul, and soul alone, that Plato wants to argue is immortal. It is not the body/soul complex of Socrates that he wishes to save, but the soul of Socrates. *Phaedo* makes this quite clear. Since every object in the world of Becoming that is visible is a soul/body composite, no visible object in the world of Becoming is itself immortal.

How can soul be immortal? I believe *Timaeus* paints the following picture. When a particular relationship is destroyed between soul and a body, then the being that was breaks down into its composite parts. The soul, freed from a relationship, would be simple at that very moment, before entering into a new relationship with other matter. There could never be a moment of destruction for it, because the destruction of the composite returns it to its pristine state. It ceases at that very moment to move a visible object and returns to the self-motion of the soul qua soul. I believe the text suggests that such self-movement is circular. Soul may be forced by the order of the cosmos to go into a new relationship with some bit of matter, but it cannot be destroyed in the process for it is simple during the process of change itself. A soul is always in its immortal form at the very moment its visible relationship is being destroyed. This is not true of the body. The body is a composite, made up of a combination of things. It begins to decay at the moment of separation.

What is the textual evidence for such a picture? It is quite compelling. The best example in the text of this process is found in the death of humans. The human body/soul composite at death breaks along its most natural fault line. Soul comes free from the body.[45] This picture of death is held throughout the Platonic corpus. *Phaedo* 64c makes quite clear,

> We believe, do we not, that death is the separation of the soul from the body, and the state of being dead is the state in which the body is separated from the soul and exists alone by itself.

This cleavage of soul from body leaves the soul by itself. A soul not in contact with body can be simple. This allows the soul to be in a relationship with a body that produces complex motions while still retaining the potential simplicity that it needs for immortality. The description of death in both *Timaeus* and *Phaedo* support this reading.

Strictly speaking, the soul in a body/soul complex is not simple. It has the mere potential for simplicity, but this simplicity is actualized only at the exact moment when it is needed. Plato has solved his problem with simplicity and motion in both the cosmic and human animal. Of course, in the cosmic animal, since there is nothing outside of it and no divine will to destroy it, this death of the body is only theoretical.

How does this relationship work in the cosmological account? What work does it do? I will only touch on some of the issues involved that will be important in the closer examination of the human soul. Soul has the cosmological function of imparting motion to a body or an animal. Of course, in a study of human psychology one is most interested in the motion imparted to a given animal. This animal might have many different types of matter that have many different appropriate types of motion. The soul, which in itself is circular motion, provides these appropriate motions. It comes into unique relationships with matter. These relationships in themselves cannot be immortal. Later I will turn to the way a human soul can produce the appropriate motions. I will also closely examine the soul's relationship with matter.

As part of the animals' being, one half of the soul/body construct, the soul would be moved with that animal in any number of directions. This relationship, and hence, the animal, cannot be immortal. Note, however, that when the animal dies, and the relationship changes, the soul would revert back to its simple function of circular motion, waiting to provide motion to another bit of matter. Soul in relation to matter moves the matter in any number of complex directions, while soul by itself is circular motion. Soul by itself is simple.[46] Soul in relation with matter is, by definition, not simple.
Death is, by definition, the breaking up of the composite, but this very process frees the soul.

Is there textual evidence that Plato viewed soul in humans or in the cosmos this way? First, Plato consistently views the soul as self-moving and the source of motion in the human and in the cosmos. In his earlier work, *Cratylus*, Plato has Socrates ask, "What is that which holds and carries and gives life and motion to the entire nature of the body? What else but the soul?"[47] In his last work, at *Laws* 895e10, he makes the same point. In speaking of the soul, the Athenian says, "But there is something that, having moved itself, alters another, and that other another, and thus thousands upon tens of thousand of things moved come into being . . ."[48] Plato clearly believed the soul was self-moving and also moved the human body.

Is the motion of the soul qua soul circular for Plato? First, it must be remembered that if the soul is to be AS simple, and hence immortal, then its motion must also be simple. It must not have a multitude of motions. Which motion would that be? In fact, Plato is clear that there is one motion he regards as best and most rational: the circular.[49] How could the soul have any other motion as its natural or default motion? If it is self-moving, as he states in many different dialogues, then this motion must be circular.

Why is this not stated more clearly in the text? The difficulty in picturing this default circular motion is, that in reality, except for the moment of death in animals, there is never an actual time in which any soul is without some body. One never observes the cosmic soul acting without a body. The two creation accounts in *Timaeus* both speak as if soul and body came into existence, but this is a creation in words and not in fact.

One must recall Plato's clear warning that both creation accounts seem to do things in a particular order, but that creation was not in time. Time was, after all, made at the incarnation of the soul in the cosmic body.[50] The creation of the cosmic soul and the cosmic body must have taken place, therefore, at the first moment of the creation of the cosmos. As T.M. Robinson expressed it, "It was a pre-time, time."[51] The cosmic soul is, therefore, always incarnate for Plato. The human soul, at the moment of death, seems to be the only exception to this rule of universal incarnation.[52] I will have more to say about the issue of time shortly.

The text does, however, give as clear an image of the natural circularity of the soul as one could expect in it discussion of the cosmic soul. The motion of the soul is most circular at the very areas of the cosmos where the matter is most fine and least concentrated. The places where humanity sees soul with the most excellent matter are in the heavens.[53] More geometrically complex, or more dense, matter brings with it more complex relationships and other motions.[54] One can, therefore, infer that the motion most like that of the non-incarnate soul would be the motion of the Same in the astral realm. I believe that Aristotle may lend support to this reading in his discussion of the *Timaeus* in *de Anima*. Aristotle says, "the resolutions of the heavens are regarded as the motions of the souls."[55]

Finally, the text supports the notion that it is placing soul in relationship to matter that produces the other motions. When the text speaks of the division of the cosmic soul at 36d to produce bands of motion within the cosmic order, Plato (as translated by Bury) speaks of the Demiurge encompassing the bands with motion. At 36d, the Demiurge appoints different motions to the different spheres. The Demiurge directs a circular motion already found in the soul by placing it into contact with different types of matter.[56] Plato makes it clear in several places that it is this contact with matter that changes or confuses the simple motions of the rational soul.[57] This picture will have obvious implications for human soul/body relationships.

So far as the text is concerned, the soul is never free of matter. It moves from one relationship to another within the world of Becoming. Why, therefore, is one relationship to be preferred to another? Plato clearly thinks of some relationships as more divine than others.[58] I think the answer lies in the nature of the soul qua soul.

Simple motions, single motions, allow the soul to do the least unnatural moving. It comes the closest to the soul's ideal of being utterly free of matter and simple in its motions. A being, like a star, that travels in only one motion, like that of the soul qua soul, is better than a being like a planet, with its retrograde motions, that travels in two. Both astral bodies are, however, superior to the combination with matter in the terrestrial realm where as many as seven motions, sometimes all at once, may be appropriate. The cosmos is as good as it can be, not perfectly good. The soul, as a part of the cosmic animal, can never for long be in the ideal state of being simply soul, self-motion in a circle. It can only be in better or worse states in this world of Becoming. It is, however, immortal. It can never escape from this cycle, unless the Demiurge Himself were to unmake the cosmic animal. Since this would be an evil act, soul will never be able to escape from the animal and the world of Becoming.

Plato has, therefore, given the reader an explanation for motion, while at the same time preserving a simple and immortal soul at the moment when he needs it. As it confronts different stuff under different circumstances, the self-movement of the soul generates different motions in matter.[59]

At 43b, Plato will describe the human soul as being confused in its motions when it comes into contact with a body. This fits nicely with the picture developed on the basis of examination of the cosmic soul. Complex motions, like those in the human body, can now be explained. Human soul in contact with certain matter cannot maintain its natural motion. Certain bits of matter have a potential motion unlike the rational circularity of the soul qua soul. It therefore confuses the normal functioning of the soul in a manner that the fire of the original astral home of the human soul does not.

The discussion of soul and motion has brought an important distinction in the Platonic psychology to light. It is important to keep this distinction clear when looking at a particular passage:

1. Soul by itself is movement in a rational, or circular direction.
2. Soul combined with matter moves in the most rational possible manner (This motion is not always circular).

It is appropriate for Plato to describe soul of the second sort moving in all sorts of directions, but to write of soul of the first sort as simple and one. One must be careful to determine the state of the soul of which Plato is speaking.

In this regard, one can quickly note that in a cosmological account Plato will almost always be dealing with soul in an incarnate stage. It will therefore most often be soul of the second sort about which he speaks. The reader should not therefore expect Plato to directly describe the soul as an independent thing.

Cosmic Soul: Some Final Reflections

It is now possible to give an overview of the Platonic psychology found in the section of the text stretching from 34b to 36c that deals with the creation of the cosmic soul. My comments in this regard are, of course, limited to those features that are relevant to a further exploration of the human psychology.

In the section beginning at 34b, Plato gives an overview of the creation and function of the cosmic soul. This cosmic soul consists of soul proper in relationship with the visible. In 34c to just before 36c (ending with κατανηλώκει), he gives the two-part description of the formation of the cosmic soul. First, in the section extending from 34c to 35b (ending with μεμειγμένην), Plato forces three disparate parts together to form soul proper. Plato has a basic understanding of mixture that allows this new unified substance to be like both the Same and the Different. This is possible in the manner (in Plato's physics) that one mixed wine may be like both of the parent wines in important ways.

Second, in 35b to 36c, he brings the cosmic soul into being by taking the AS soul and relating it to the visible. The cosmic soul is drawn to continue the motion of the Same when it becomes incarnate in the proper matter for that motion.[60] It is drawn into the motion of the Different when it comes into contact with matter that has the potential to be moved in the motion of the Different. The cosmic soul is, therefore, AS simple in itself, but has a series of complex relationships with the visible, material world. This soul behaves in a complex manner based on the reaction of different matter to the cosmic soul's nature. Soul without matter would not move in a complex manner. It would remain that which is simply self-movement in a circular motion.

At 36c and following, Plato begins his description of the function of that cosmic soul in the universe. It is not my purpose to describe the relationship and functions of the cosmic soul within the universe. These functions include the ability of the cosmic animal to reason. This is an important topic, but outside of the scope of this investigation. It is enough to argue that the soul qua soul can be thought of as simple. Since my purpose is to describe the functioning of the human soul, a description of the interesting and complex interactions of the cosmic soul with the cosmic body and the Forms must be deferred to another work. It will be important for my description of Plato's human psychology to keep in mind the two ways that Plato may use soul. He may be referring to the AS simple soul or to the complex soul that in its interactions with matter causes complex motions. The AS simple soul is usually only discussed in relationship to the human soul at death.

Time and the Soul

Plato moves from this discussion of the creation of the cosmic soul to the description of the creation of time. This includes the genesis of the astral bodies in their appropriate places. This section is important for my purposes mainly to shed light on the so-called order of creation. It suggests that the cosmic soul and the cosmic body were formed simultaneously. Time came into being with their motion in harmonious relationship. The soul might still be ontologically prior, but it will necessarily have no chronological priority.

Plato often speaks as if the soul is prior to the body in other dialogues. This priority would seem to be not just in terms of superiority, but in terms of causation. For example, in *Philebus*, Plato has Socrates argue that reason, which is found in the most excellent soul, is the chief cause of things. This would seem to be an argument for temporal priority and not just ontological priority. Now, of course, following the initial moment of creation, when both soul and body exist, all future actions can have soul as their cause. Yet soul appears to be the cause of body in all things, including the creative act. What can be made of this apparent conflict?

I would suggest that it is adequate for Plato's purposes if the soul, including the human soul, has the appearance of such a causal history without actually possessing such a history.[61] Plato is concerned to preserve the priority of the soul over the body and for him such priority is only given to the firstborn. In reality, both body and soul as a functioning unit are created or exist together. What does it mean for the soul to have the appearance of a history without actually having such a history? I would formalize the notion in the following manner:

1. For functional reasons, both the cosmic body and the cosmic soul (CB and CS) came into being at the same time (t1).[62]
2. For any object O in the CB, if O has a temporal cause, then O was caused by CS.
3. Any object O caused by CS has, therefore, a history.
4. For every object O, O appears to have a temporal cause that creates an appearance of a history for that object O.
5. At the moment of creation t1, no state of affairs S existed in the actual world W such that O could not have been created with the appearance of history.
6. Therefore: At t1 for any object O, it would appear that O existed or was caused at t1-n.
7. Therefore: (with x and n standing for any given amount of time) At t1 or t1+x the appearance of history in an object O which makes it appear that O existed at (t1 or t1+x)- n, is not equivalent to O existing at (t1 or t1+x)- n.
8. Therefore: Any object O that appears to have history did not necessarily exist at each moment in that history.
9. From 1: The universe did not exist prior to t1.
10. Therefore: CB, which has an apparent history of t1-n, did not actually exist at t1-n.

Let me summarize the argument. There is no way, using observation alone, to differentiate between an apparent history for an object and its actual history. Cosmic soul, and the souls of all humans, will always appear to come before and cause their respective bodies. The particular scientific myth of the astronomer, and certain features of the component parts of reality she has deduced using her best reason, may cause her to postulate that body and soul-system actually came into being at some discrete time together. Alternately, she might speculate that body and soul have always existed in a mutual coming-to-be relationship.

For example, the astronomer may believe that only the Forms can exist eternally and that the world of Becoming and hence its constituent parts is a coming-to-be thing. Such an astronomer, like Timaeus, may therefore postulate a continuous beginning point for both body and soul. This continuous beginning point (any time t) would never be apparent on the basis of looking at the world of Becoming alone. Of course, the astronomer need not be able to pick out any given moment of time for this beginning. Any time will do. At that time, soul will look like it has existed at "t-1" as the cause of the body. In short, Plato's universe with the soul and the body created at the same time must have the appearance of a history that is not actual. A theoretical outside observer looking at the cosmos would sensibly assume a causal chain that stretched beyond the first moment of time.

In other dialogues, therefore, it would make sense to speak of the soul as causing all features within the body of the cosmos or of even a first human. This would be a good and reasonable conclusion, in fact the only conclusion, that could be reached by looking only at the features of the world of Becoming. To say anything else would be, for Plato, to go beyond the data at hand. Only with the advent of the mythic examination of the details of the relationship between the cosmic body and the cosmic soul does new information come to light. Only the careful astronomer Timaeus has the grounds for stating that the cosmos has a continuous beginning that is not the same as appearance.

Plato can, therefore, without confusion, speak in one dialogue as if the soul has temporal priority as unaided science must assume and in another dialogue as if body and soul came into being together. By using the notion of apparent history, Plato can have a notion of soul that has functional priority and the appearance of temporal priority. This soul, however, need not have actually existed before the body in order to achieve this status.

What does the text say about this suggestion? Does the *Timaeus* itself demand the interpretation that soul and body came into being together? Perhaps it would be simpler to reinterpret the text to support the notion that the creation of the soul came before that of the body. Cornford and many other commentators tend to treat the creation of the visible cosmos as if it came to pass after the formation of the soul in actuality and not just in words.[63] The text itself gives indirect, but convincing evidence that both the soul and the body of the cosmos were created together. The *Timaeus* at 37e states that time was created with the appearance of motion. It also declares that the Creator made the planets to act as a means to measure time. As Cornford describes it, celestial bodies become the cosmic clock.[64] The Creator wants it to be possible to count the progression of time. Since matter cannot move without soul, motion per se cannot exist without soul. The soul is necessary for a body to have the ability to move. Therefore, the soul either came into being with the body and time or before the body and time.

The natural tendency is to assume, as do Cornford and Taylor, that the soul came into being before the body. There is the less interesting sense where this is, of course, impossible. Time and hence chronology came into being with the formation of the soul. There was no time before the formation of the body. T.M. Robinson suggested in a private conversation with me that this might suggest a Platonic speculation regarding a pre-time time. This notion, of course, suggests some contemporary theorizing in modern physics. I will use time language in this discussion, therefore, to refer to some other time, the Robinson pre-cosmic time in which he believes the soul came into being. In fact, I hope to demonstrate that such a reading is not the best way to handle the text.

Robinson and others have what appears to be clear textual support on their side. Timaeus says at 34c that the soul is elder (πρεσβύτερον) and "first in birth" (καὶ γενέσει). His concern is to establish that the soul is not inferior to the body. In civil and religious thinking in the Greek world, the elder child had certain rights and authority in domestic relationships. In describing the world, Plato had understandably begun with the familiar visible world and moved to the more abstract world of the Forms. Plato was worried that this positioning of the visible world's description would leave the impression with the reader that the visible world held the elder position in the cosmic order. He denies this in the passage at 34c.

I would, however, argue that the description "first and most excellent in birth" be taken to refer to the nature of the genesis of the soul, and its apparent history in relationship to the body, and not to the actual time of the soul's development. It was common to speak of rulers as the fathers of their country. Thus a young man in a position of authority might be the father of all of his chronological elders in a city. His birth was first in quality if not in chronology. Since he is using words, the writer must deal with things in a particular order. The best order to use in describing creation that would facilitate comprehension on the part of the reader is to begin with the visible and to move to the invisible. The best order to aid in understanding the comparative excellence of the soul and the body is to move in the other direction. In fact, cosmic soul and cosmic body were created simultaneously, but the soul was the first or most excellent creation.

I am not suggesting, of course, that Plato must be using the idea of firstborn to merely describe excellence and not chronological order. The more traditional reading is still possible. However, why speculate that Plato was hinting at a concept that was unknown until Christian theology and the most recent advances in physics? A natural reading of the text is available that allows the reader to understand the passage within the context of the ideas of the time. It is true that Plato could have been far ahead of his time, but why assume this if there is a less anachronistic reading of the passage? The notion of an apparent history, making sense of the appearance of priority of the soul, is a natural development of the language of appearance and time within the text.

Plato, in fact, gives the reader further textual reasons to believe that the soul and the body are created together. His use of the term heaven (ου'ρανὸν) in 34b is most revealing. He uses ου'ρανὸν 'ενα μόνον ε''ρημον (one solitary heaven) to describe the completed soul and body construct. This heaven is pronounced a "blessed God." At 36e, Plato refers to the "body of the heaven" and to the soul permeating the heaven. It is clear that neither the cosmic soul or the body are heaven for Plato. They are each part of heaven or the seat of the god. Plato is using the term in a unique and special way to describe the entire cosmic order.

The critical passages at 37e-39e must be understood in this context. Plato deals time and again in this passage with heaven. He directly states that time came into existence with the heaven. There is no reason to read this statement as referring to anything other than to the soul/body composite. Time came into being with the composite heaven. Its progress was marked off by the motions of the visible bodily planets. The early sections of the text (37d-38b) deal, therefore, with the coming of time. The later passages (38b-39e) deal with the physical means given to humankind to mark off time. If this reading is adopted, then the problem of the putative order of creation is settled. One should never force an anachronistic reading on Plato, when an alternative is available. The notion of a pre-time time breaks this sensible rule.

Plato concludes this section at 40e by finishing up the details of the creation of the cosmic animal. This work is not sequential. It is easiest to use sequential language to describe such events. Humankind cannot easily continue to think about multiple events that occur at the same time. This is a sequence in words and not in actuality.

It is not my intention to discuss the work of the Creator in forming the body of the cosmic animal.[65] One textual point will, however, be critical to later arguments. The Creator fashions a body to function at each level of the universal order. The four cosmic "psycho-systems"[66] are the realm of the astral bodies, the realm of the air, the realm of the land, and the realm of the body. The astral bodies are motivated by the intelligence, the cosmic soul, that I have described earlier. They are declared to be divine. In the next major section of the dialogue, the Father/Creator will give these divine beings the task of creating a human.

To summarize, I have argued that Plato can sensibly picture the cosmos as coming into being as a soul/body composite. This soul/body composite will have the appearance of history that would lead those not fully informed to think that the soul must come before the body in actuality. The soul has priority over the body for Plato based on its causal priority and on the apparent cosmic history. The fact that both in actuality came into being together does not argue against this. This is important to human psychology, because humankind can exist from eternity as body/soul composites while still sensibly speaking about the priortiy of the soul. Since most of the Platonic myths seem to assume an almost infinite antiquity for humankind, this idea has decent textual support.[67]

The Creation of a Unified Human Soul

Having examined the formation of the cosmic soul, Plato now turns to the formation of the human soul at 41b. This is the key part of the dialogue for the project of understanding Plato's human psychology. *Timaeus* illuminates this psychology through a discussion of its origins and functions within the world of Becoming.

Plato introduces the topic with a long set of instructions on the part of the Demiurge to the gods. In a passage that will later be critical to my picture of the soul in *Timaeus,* the Demiurge says, "Ye gods, those gods whose maker I am and those works whose father I am, being created by me are indissoluble without my consent. Anything bonded together can of course be dissolved, though only an evil will would consent to dissolve anything whose composition and state were good."[68]

At this point in the dialogue, Plato turns to the central issue for my argument as he describes the creation of the human soul. The human soul is composed of the same substances that went into making the universal soul. The substances used in forming the human soul are somehow less pure then those used in making the universal soul. A.E.

Taylor describes this process as the creation of a "second or third vintage." The human soul is not equivalent to the cosmic soul in terms of its excellence.

The reader is forced to ask, "From whence did this material come?" In the previous description of the making of the cosmic soul, the material used was all consumed in the process. Taylor comments on this problem in the following way, "Note that they are blended directly by the hands of the Creator, and they are not made of what was left in the κρατήρ (mixing bowl)."[69] Cornford does not comment on this issue at all. Taylor's position seems possible, if one assumes that the residue from which the Creator mixed the human soul was the residue of the basic ingredients and not of the mixture used for the cosmic soul. This is, of course, made more likely by the fact that the Creator has to go through the mixing process again.

An account like that, perhaps, helps explain where the material comes from, but leaves the reader at a loss to explain why such material should be considered inferior. It is important to remember that the basic elements of the soul are the Same, the Different, and Being. How could these elements be less pure? The mixture used to form the human soul is composed of the dregs (ὑπόλοιπα) of the material used in forming the cosmic soul. Plato notes that it is no longer undefiled (ἀκήρατα). How could basic concepts be defiled?

I would like to suggest that, if my earlier reading is correct, the impurity comes from the fact that the absolute unity in mixing achieved in the cosmic soul has not been quite achieved in the human soul. The residue left behind in a mixing bowl contains elements, floating in the wine, that have not become part of the wine. In the dregs, one has the new wine and improperly mixed items. The other way to picture these dregs is as a residue that is not mixed in proper proportion to get fusion.

What does this mean? The soul formed by the Creator for humanity is like the cosmic soul in being AS simple left to itself. Of course, just as it was in the case of the cosmic soul, when the AS simple part of the human soul comes into contact with the body it will enter into a complex relationship. It is not, however, exactly like the cosmic soul because the human soul is not yet finished. The AS portion of the soul is done, but there is more to humanity than the AS soul and a body. There are portions of the human soul that were not completed by God. He leaves this completion to the lesser gods, but they cannot finish the task properly. This impurity or unfinished task is a foreshadowing of the creation by the lesser gods of the mortal soul.

God provides the demigods with a finished immortal (AS) soul with attachments that are unfinished. The demigods are to complete the blending in those unfinished parts.[70] These lesser gods complete the full human soul as best they can, but they cannot bring these dregs into full harmony. The human soul, therefore, is created with two parts: an immortal and mortal part.[71] No more will be said about the mortal part until 61c. Within the religious portions of the myth, where the work of God must be kept apart from the work of demigods, no more can be said. Of course the human soul in the context of the entire dialogue is a combined and simultaneous work of Reason (the God) and Necessity (which I take to be the work of the mythical demigods).

Why did the Creator fail to finish the task? The text at 41c indicates that if God had finished the task, the human soul would have been just like the cosmic soul. The goal, however, was for the cosmic animal to contain all and not just some types of created being. The cosmic animal with its fully rational cosmic soul represented the one extreme type of becoming. It is a becoming in the direction of reason. Matter, that is not rational, but moves by necessity of like being attracted to like in space, represents the other extreme.[72] It is a becoming in the direction of chaos. Humanity and its soul, which has both the pure and the impure in it, represents the median between these two. Humanity has both rational motion and irrational motion, the rational soul and the irrational soul.

This gives a cosmological reason for the Platonic belief that the human soul needs further purification before it achieves perfect bliss.[73] This, of course, was not the case with the cosmic soul. According to the text, the cosmic soul is made one Form. No such claim is made about the human soul. The cosmic soul is created with a total harmony, as I have argued previously. It has one creator, the most divine Demiurge. The human soul, however, goes through a clear two-part creation process. Two of its subdivisions are created by the inferior gods. The human soul is described as having a deathless, or immortal, part and a mortal part at 42e7. There is, therefore, textual justification for claiming a need for further purification in the human soul that was not available in the earlier account of the creation of the cosmic soul. There was no indication that any part of the cosmic soul was inferior to any other part.

This means that pieces of the human soul may be come undone in the process that humans call death. The dying process itself would then be understood as part of the healing and unifying needed by this inferior soul. The mortal sections would have to be re-harmonized in another life. A life lived badly means a life that will have to be lived again to continue the attempt to make the whole human soul harmonious and pure. This notion of the human soul needing further purging and work is, of course, a theme that resonates in Plato in texts ranging from the *Gorgias* 523-524 to the *Republic* 614c-621d. The *Timaeus* has, therefore, led the reader to the point of seeing the necessity for such mythological purification.

What then is the relationship between the human soul and the cosmic soul? It is not the case that the thing that functions as the human soul is as pure and undefiled as the cosmic soul is. However, such a situation need not be viewed as eternal. If impurity is viewed in a Christian sense, then it is eternal. For the Christian, the man who is no longer a virgin can never be a virgin again. If I am correct, such is not the case for Plato, despite later Christian neo-Platonic readings of these passages. For Plato, such impurity is a matter of improper mixing or of foreign elements. This gives a reason for human soul's becoming part of the material world. The human soul is having impurities removed from it. Its elements are coming into proper proportion. It is a third type of becoming in that it is not yet fully becoming in terms of reason nor fully becoming in terms of mere necessity. The goal of the individual human soul is to become like the greater cosmic soul, pure and devoted to a reasonable becoming.

It is no accident that each soul is given a star.[74] There the soul is shown the pattern of the universe.[75] Wheeling about the Earth on the circle of the Same, they learn the motion of reason.[76] This learning begins the process of completing the mixing that has been so imperfectly done in the mixing bowl. In support of this contention, the reader is told that such an implantation in the world is the result of "necessity."[77] The best possible human soul is driven to the body as result of its own imperfections.

Before incarnation, on its star the human soul is taught the nature of the world of Becoming. They are shown "the laws of destiny."[78] Most importantly, these   laws focus on the process of purification. The human soul is shown the justice of the cosmic order. Each human will get "one and the same first birth." None will be slighted by the God.[79] Human nature is revealed as two-fold. The two-fold nature, which I take to be another way of describing the unfinished portion of the soul, gives humanity the reason for incarnation. In humans, this two-fold nature is partially reflected in the division of humans into genders. Man is declared the superior sex.[80] Later, more extreme cases of a divided soul will be related to the existence of animals. More critically, the human soul is shown the confusion that will result from its incarnation and the method needed to achieve purification.

The human soul is, therefore, shown in repeated ways to be a duality. It contains an immortal part, like the cosmic soul, which left alone will move in the path of reason: circular motion. It also has a portion that is impure and will be able to receive sensations within the world of Becoming. The human soul will, therefore, be the one thing in the cosmos capable of experiencing both types of motion, both types of becoming, and choosing between them.

This AS soul is immortal and teachable. The AS soul allows the soul-complex, which Plato also calls soul, to be rational. The AS, divine, and perfect soul is embedded in a lesser soul-like construction formed by the demigods. In this sense, it is part of a construct. However, in the ideal human, it is not controlled or strongly influenced by the lesser soul. This relationship is not necessary for the immortal soul and is not intended to be a biconditional one. The immortal soul does that which it is designed to do: providing the ability for intelligent motion to the body.[81] As has been shown, it stands in a union with a mortal portion. The relationship of the two major parts of the human soul is not, however, without laws. It has the weaknesses that Plato will later (in this dialogue) attach to women. Just as humanity is composed of the well-formed male and the ill-formed female, so too the soul construct contains both the divine potential and human frailty.

This still leaves the reader with the question of why Plato made this move, so uncharacteristic of his earlier views on women found in *Republic*.[82] There is no way to finally resolve this problem. This failure on the part of Plato is a powerful argument in favor of relating the *Timaeus* to the later and more socially conservative *Laws* in terms of its actual date of composition. Plato, of course, wants to account for the fact that humans are divided by gender. If my reading is correct, then he has also developed a two-part image of the human soul. He desires a myth that will account for both of these features. He does so by reflecting the duality of the human soul in the sexual division of the human race.

Such a division, unfaithful to his better instincts, was not a necessary move on his part. Plato might have tied the ill-formed soul to genetic physical defects. This is, perhaps, only a marginal improvement from the point of view of contemporary ethics. A more socially conservative view of humanity seems to have overtaken Plato later in his life. The old idealism of the *Republic* is not carried forward at this point. Since the two dialogues are so closely linked, the clear statement of female inferiority found at 42 might be viewed as a retraction of the image painted in *Republic*.

Plato has now developed the purely psychological picture of the origin of the human race in great detail. Humans in the world of Becoming are not, however, mere disembodied souls. From the beginning of the dialogue, he has stressed the incarnation of the soul in a body. What is the relationship of the soul to this body?

The Soul and Body Relationship

Introduction to the Problem

Plato must account for all the features of a human. He owes the reader an account of the formation and function of the human body. He also must develop the relationship between that body and the human soul.

How does Plato describe the human body and its formation? A brief review of a few of the details will facilitate a fresh approach to the relationship between body and soul. The divine Creator has nothing to do with the formation of the human bodies. He removes himself from any possible imputation of injustice. The gods are allowed to create the mortal body as the seat for the "deathless" ($\alpha'\theta\acute{\alpha}\nu\alpha\tau\alpha$[83]) soul. The human soul is, then, handed over to the gods. The gods structure a body for the soul. "They copied the shape of the universe and fastened the two divine orbits (Same and Different) into a spherical body, which we now call a head, the divinest part of us which controls all the rest...." [84] What is the impact of the soul on the body?

This addition of a body throws the soul into confusion. Each soul is born into the world, at the appropriate time, in a male body. The soul experiences great trauma and confusion, because of its contact with the movements of the world of Becoming. It forgets the great truths it learned in the realm of the stars. The ordered motions of both the Same and the Different are confused. It becomes capable, therefore, of making errors of judgement. The human soul becomes like the "upside down man"[85] whose vision and judgements about left and right are reversed. His mind is in a literal muddle. This absolute irrationality is always found in the infant, but decreases in intensity with the decline in growth and experience that comes with age.

Education can help the soul at the point when growth begins to taper off. The soul can, thereby, escape "the worst of maladies."[86] If the soul allows passion to govern it, then it suffers loss, makes errors, and is reincarnated in a woman's body. To continue to give in to the passions of the flesh, to allow the impurities of the human soul to continue, would cause the soul to be planted in the body of a wild beast. Only if the soul defeats passion will it return to its starry chariot. The soul is to recapture the motion of the Same, as much as possible in its bodily form, in order to regain its best astral home. Timaeus makes it clear that even physical illness can bring disorders to the soul. This relationship shows the close connection between body and soul.[87]

This brief overview of Plato's picture of the body-soul-system faces many difficulties. Why are humans so imperfect if they are the products of divine Reason? How do the soul and the body relate on a physical level? How does the soul produce motion in the body? How is the body able to have such a negative impact on the soul? Partial answers to these questions have already been given. A careful examination of this portion of the *Timaeus* will shed even more light on these problems.

Necessity and the Relationship of Body and Soul

Why is the human less than perfect? Why can't the demigods produce an ideal being? Plato must confront the tension between the observable imperfections of the human being and his desire to have a creature that is the product of reason and goodness. At 48e, Plato moves the dialogue forward in a novel manner in an attempt to solve these and other problems. He has been describing the working of Reason or Intelligence in the world. Now he admits a second formative concept into the picture. Necessity, the unavoidable perversity of the natural world, has to be dealt with. As Plato points out at 48, the world has been a compromise between intelligence and necessity from the start. The world is the best possible world, not the best world. As a result, things come into being that would not exist if the world were the pure work of reason. This will be of vital importance for understanding the full nature of the human soul. The imperfect soul of the mixing bowl which is the product of divine intelligence will be further modified through the constraints of necessity within the physical world. Reason must persuade Necessity. The divine cannot do without the base. It also cannot simply tell the base how it should be.

What is the explanation for this inability on the part of reason? Plato has earlier divided the universe into two parts: the World of

Being and the world of Becoming. The World of Being, eternal, unchanging and divine, is to be duplicated in the world of Becoming. The difficulty, which Plato describes using powerful imagery in this section, is that the world of Becoming never fully is. For the craftsman to build an image of the world of the Forms, he must work with a material that has no attributes in itself and never comes into full being. It is always coming into being and so any outcome is unpredictable. The Demiurge is building with a material that is itself in the process of coming into existence. The gods can guide such a process, but they cannot control it. The individual thing within that world can therefore only be shaped for a short time as the space or plastic becomes first one thing and then another. The craftsman can never finish his work. It is always slipping away into something else.

The soul of the mixing bowl can be created apart from the demands of necessity because it is not yet out in the world of Becoming. This makes possible the creation of both the cosmic soul and the immortal, rational part of the human soul. Even at this point, however, the God must create it with that future interaction in mind. The human soul will have to face the sensible world. The soul that can sense the changing objects of the world of Becoming is the mortal soul. The full creation of that soul can be delayed, as has already been noted, until the demi-gods/gods bring it into full contact with the physical world.

No object of the visible, physical world has such a luxury. It is, in every part and detail, a compromise between the harsh demands of Necessity and the persuasive words of Reason. Plato again stresses that only an account of the first things, the Forms, could be a certain account. At 48d, he invokes the gods to aid him and attempts to give a likely account. This time he will describe the formation of the physical universe.

Since creation of both the soul and the physical universe actually occur at the same time, Plato begins his account of creation again. He introduces at this point that strange concept of the ὑποδοχὴν (receptacle).[88] This space [89] allows Plato to differentiate between the four traditional Greek elements by geometric arrangement. The physical world is described as being in a constant state of flux. Plato's account, with his Forms having Parmenidean stability and his material world in a Heraclitean flux, is a fine synthesis of the arguments of the earlier Greek philosophers. Plato has started to explain the reasons for the imperfections in humanity, but he has yet to explain how soul and body work together.

Relationships within the Parts of the Human: Motion in the Soul/Body Composite

At this point in the development of the Platonic psychology, it is important to ask what the relationship is between the physical body and the soul-system of Plato. What is going on in the text up to 70? Plato has pictured humans with three basic elements: a body, a mortal soul, and an immortal soul. He will later provide more detail about two of the elements, but the basic picture will remain the same. How do the divine soul, the mortal soul, and the body work together?

First, it is clear that all three are in relationship. They can have an impact on each other. Whatever the ideal relationship should be, in practice each of these members of the human organism can impact the other. I have already mentioned that even the immortal, and originally simple, divine soul can be confused by the improper motions of the body. The mortal soul is able to be made sick by the disorders of the body.

It seems there are two relationships that exist for the human being. One is the ideal state of the soul that functions exactly as the Demiurge and the gods would have it function. The other is the relationship that humans actually have from the moment of birth onward. In the ideal state, the human being is composed of an immortal soul which has, by its very nature, rational motion. Hence, each human has the basis for ordered reason within the body. This circular motion of the immortal soul contacts the mortal elements of the soul-system and initiates the passions associated with them. Plato will give a further description of these elements and emotions later in the dialogue. The body is driven by the mortal soul to fulfill the demands of reason. The human, thus put together, will develop in the optimum manner toward satisfying his or her role in the cosmic harmony. The relationship moves, therefore, from the finest and most excellent portion to the crudest and least important portion. It would never, in a just human being, be appropriate for the better to be subordinate to the lesser and so this relationship should always be one way.

This is a completely intellectual picture of the human being. The AS simple or immortal[90] soul, in its contact with the world through the mortal soul and the body, should not be changed by that impact. It does not ideally receive anything from them, but it moves them constantly toward order while preserving its own rational motion. Human beings would, therefore, shape the world around them, or at the very least not be changed by it. They would gain this ability through the circular motion of the immortal soul.

The immortal human soul would, like the cosmic soul, be such that it would cause motion when it came into contact with a particular substance. At this point, the earlier discussion of motion in the cosmos becomes quite helpful. *Timaeus* 37a-c describe the results of the union of an immortal/rational human soul and a body. The body is moved by the soul in a manner that is appropriate to it.[91] The soul which is moving with the body in the new soul-body relationship knows the nature of the body by the motion that has been brought about in the union of the two. Plato has, therefore, gained a simple physical account for intellectual activity.

The basic nature of soul never changes. It always is self-moved and it always attempts a circular motion. However, not every material object in the universe has the potential to be moved in circles. Earth, for example, has seemingly no natural tendency to move in circles. It is a becoming thing that has the tendency to move toward other earth, most of which is "down." This happens for no rational reason, but only because "like is attracted to like." Soul cannot, therefore, always fulfill its own natural motion. In contact with sufficient amounts of matter not inclined to circular motion like earth, human soul may in fact be overwhelmed.[92] It may then unite with the matter in a motion that is not like its own natural motion.

If a human soul is, at the moment, providing for the actualization of a circular motion in a certain body and the body changes such that now soul can only induce a vertical motion (because of the strong inclination of the body), then soul has entered into a changed relationship with the body. This changed motion will be recognized by the soul. This recognition is the key to intellectual activity in the human.

In this manner, the soul can differentiate between the objects with which it comes into contact. The soul enters into changing relationships with matter. It is impacted by those relationships in terms of the direction of its motion. A simple cosmological example will clarify the relationship. Things made of star stuff have the potential to move in the motion of the Same if placed in intercourse with the cosmic soul. Things made of planet stuff have the potential to move with the motion of the Different. In the first case, the soul is able to move in its natural motion. Matter is defined as that which can be moved by soul.

The AS human soul, the immortal soul created by the

Demiurge, is in contact with the mortal soul created by the gods. The mortal soul is in contact with the body. The body is in contact with the rest of the world of Becoming. In a proper human being, the motions of the entire human being are generated in directions appropriate to their substance by the immortal AS soul. That which should move in the direction of the Same, the brain, is motivated by the immortal soul to do so. When a brain comes into contact with a thing outside itself, this thing receives its appropriate motion or motions from the soul. This allows the ideal human to correctly identify the objects with which it comes into contact.

Of course, the ideal human is not the sort of human that often exists in the world of Becoming. As I have shown, the world of Becoming cannot take a final impression from the work of the craftsman. The relationships in a world that never ceases the process of becoming are inherently unstable. The gods may will one thing, but the flux within the space will modify their intention. Within the head of any given human being, the changing, becoming substance of the world overwhelms the proper motions of the immortal soul.

The immortal soul is still potentially able to restore proper motion to itself and the body. It is important to remember that soul as soul is unchanging in its primary characteristic. It is always striving to return to its natural self-moving circular path. The many ephemeral substances of becoming, with their own chaotic desire to move to other like substance without reason, can suppress this natural tendency. It is important to recall that humans only see souls when they are in combination with bodies. Most of the time on the Earth, one sees soul in combination with matter that is complex and dense. Humans rarely see soul acting in it natural capacity. This explains the importance of astronomy. In fact vision, the chief physical cause is explained by Plato in terms of allowing for the art of astronomy at *Timaeus* 47b-c.

Plato places the art of astronomy in first place amongst the blessings of secondary or physical causes. Out of astronomy comes philosophy. Of course this once again affirms Timaeus, the astronomer, as a worthy guide.[93] The ultimate use of vision is the redemption of the human soul. The philosopher gazes at the stars in order to harmonize the motions of his own soul with the motions of the stars.

How does this work? The astronomer is able to see in the heavens, where matter is less dense, the proper motion of the soul-circular and continuous self-movement. He is able to recognize that this is better than the disordered motion of the lower Earth. As "like is drawn to like" so the natural motion of his soul, however confused, has the ability to recognize in the astral plane that which it longs to perform. Any human can always recollect this very fact from the Laws taught to him by the God.

This vision of the astral realm, and the longing set up in his immortal soul for such motion, gives a confused human the first clue to bringing the motions of his mind into right order. The astronomical phenomenon serve as a constant reminder of the proper motion of soul. Of course, merely gazing at these motions will not solve his problems, as Socrates points out in *Republic*.[94] It is not looking up or staring at things, even stars, that is helpful. As Plato says in *Republic,* one might as well stare at the ceiling if that is all that is happening. It is the recognition of the proper motion of the stars, the motion of the Same, and the ordering of time that is vital to the start of philosophy. Astronomy is the art that guarantees that the human soul will able to recollect what it has learned from the God on the astral plane. Of course, this turn to astronomy may explain how the soul can begin to recover from improper motion, but still not fully explain the existence of such improper motions. The chief problem for human psychology develops when the divine and unchanging AS soul fails to provide the proper motion to the human body.

How could this be? How can soul fail to produce proper motion in the mind of a human? Plato is not clear on this point. He uses metaphorical language to refer to the AS soul being confused by the overwhelming motions of the rest of the body and the mortal soul. At 72d, Plato makes it clear that the divisions of the soul and its placement in the human body are not something he feels he can know for certain. The reason for this is obvious. When Plato dealt with the creation of the immortal soul, he was dealing with the creation of the thing closest to the ideal World of Being. It was possible, with careful thought, to know things about such an object. The moment that ideal soul became caught in the world of Becoming, such knowledge became impossible. True knowledge of the relationship of the immortal soul to the body and mortal soul is impossible. He does affirm, however, that his picture is the most probable account.

I believe that the description of the soul up to 70 in the text does leave a possible answer to the problem. I have alluded to it in my brief discussion of motion. It is now time to explore that relationship in more detail. In short, I believe that the immortal soul fails to provide proper motion to the mortal soul and the body because it only has the ability to provide proper motion in a finite amount of substance at any given time.

Plato at 57 and following provides for a directional impulse in the universe. The physical world is placed inside the cosmic sphere. When matter that has a soul comes into contact with the boundries of the sphere there is an inward impulse. Soul provides the motion, but the border provides pressure to move inward. Like a bullet bouncing off a wall, the elements with soul contact this boundry and recoil in an inward direction. This pressure results in the blending of the component parts of the cosmos. Fire, for example, is sharp and is forced down into areas where it would not naturally go. It then attempts to return to its appropriate level, the outer region of the sphere. All the elements are involved in this process. This is conjoined with the natural tendency of "like to like."[95] The entire set of motions caused by these natural drives form part of the natural order and cannot end. Cornford describes this as a shift to a mechanical cause of motion. He explains it as the necessary physical result of the packing of the physical world within the cosmic sphere.[96] I believe the motive force still comes from soul, but that there are natural impulses caused by soul coming into contact with different matter or the edge of the cosmos that disturbed the normal, preferred direction of the soul. Plato refers in a loose manner to these natural impulses as "motion," but they are not motion strictly speaking. Earth without soul would not move anywhere. Earth with soul desires circular motion and desires to move toward other earth. One tendency in earth cooperates with soul and the other resists.

The soul placed inside the cosmic sphere comes into contact with these natural impulses. In a sense, it must overcome them to both impart and possess its proper motion. The star fire would naturally and mechanistically desire to move upward. The soul manages to keep it in the proper circular motion. It is able to overcome what must be a relatively weak mechanistic impulse to move up. Why cannot it do this in the human brain?

The immortal soul in the human skull is in a much denser part of the universe in terms of materials. There is more matter with which it can come into contact. This matter is in a constant motion that may not be proper to it. The soul in the lower realm would, therefore, come into contact with a greater diversity of substance[97] and hence a large number of motions.[98] Both of these distractions are made clear at 43b (Bury translation) where Plato says,

> For while the flood which foamed in and streamed out was immense, still greater was the tumult produced within each creature as a result of the colliding bodies, when the body of a creature happened to meet

and collide with alien fire from without, or with a solid lump of earth or liquid glidings of waters, or when it was overtaken by a tempest of winds driven by air, and when the motions due to all these causes rushing through the body impinged upon the soul.

Note that the diversity of matter as a cause of the confusion of the soul is not the same as the motion of the soul. For example, soul contacting earth is compelled by necessity to move the earth toward other earth. The motion comes from the soul, the directional impulse from the nature of earth.

In the upper regions, the soul would generally come into contact only with the star fire. The problem of the overwhelmed human soul is, therefore, solved by postulating that any given piece of the Platonic AS soul is not capable of moving every type of substance or great amounts of substance and still retaining its natural motion.[99] It can be confronted with so much becoming stuff and so much contrary "motion"[100] that it fails to maintain its natural motion. Any given bit of soul has limited power to follow its natural course. This is evident from the fact that it is confused, though it still maintains some hope for restoration. It would seem from the text that this dangerous concentration of motions and matter is reached only below the orbit of the planets.

This position could be clarified in the following manner:

1. Any immortal soul (S) attempts to move in a circular motion (C).[101]

2. For any given element x, if S is joined to x, then S will move with x in C, if S can give C to x.[102]

3. For each element x at a location l, there is a "sorting motion" m that x possesses as a result of being at l.[103]

4. There exists some amount n of sorting motions m, such that S cannot move in C with x if l contains n m's.[104]

5. There may exist some amount N of element x, such that S cannot give C to x if l contains N x's, but S can give C to x at l if the amount of m's at l is n-1 and the amount of x's at l is N-1.[105]

6. There may exist some types of elements E, such that S cannot give C to E.[106]

7. If a soul cannot impart C to E or x, then it will still impart some other motion (Z) to E or x.[107]

Therefore:

1. For every given element x, S will move x C if and only if, the amount of m's at l is < or = n-1 (condition M) and the amount of x's at l is < or = N-1 (condition X) or x is not E.
2. For every element x, S will move x C if and only if x is M and X and not E.

Relevant observations from the text:

1. Every object x in the astral sphere has M and X and is not E.[108]
2. There is an object B (the human brain), such that B can possess M and X and not E within the human body.[109]
3. For any given part of the human body that is not B, then B cannot possess M and X.[110]

If this view of the interaction of the Soul and the rest of the human is correct, then one would expect that Plato will suggest reducing n and N. How might this be done? A desire to reduce N in the body might lead to fasting and abstaining from any activity that would increase the amount of negative types of substance in the body. Does Plato advocate this? He does at 70e and 76b, where he points out the disruption brought to the soul by the eating of food. He also mentions that certain foodstuffs like wine can disrupt the soul.[111] The further desire to reduce n, the number of motions confronting a human soul, is behind the praise of astronomy that was found in earlier portions of the text. I will examine Plato's prescription for the healthy soul in more detail later. It is enough for now to note that this way of looking at the immortal soul, mortal soul, and body interaction fits those later portions of the text.

This way of looking at the human soul is important to the Platonic psychology for two reasons. First, the immortal soul continues to exist within a human, even though it may be unable to do its work. Soul can be made impotent by the density and diversity of the substance and motions it is supposed to counteract. Second, it provides some hope that the human immortal soul can prevail over this difficulty. If the mortal soul and the body can be brought to the point of being in right order, where they are not overwhelming the immortal soul with the matter and motion of the universe, then a human being can hope to gain the best possible physical state.[112]

One final point should be made before leaving this portion of the Platonic explanation of motion within the human soul. Plato has provided an analysis of motion and being that might serve as a pattern for examining the force of contemporary ideas like the blind watch maker thesis in modern biology as it applies to human origins. There is a possible co-existence of purposeful and intelligent sources of motion with motion that behaves in irrational and law-like ways. The two need not be mutually exclusive.[113]

The Body and Soul: A New Element

What of the impure or less finished parts of the human soul? At 61d, during Plato's discussion of the structure of bodies, the reader encounters a pivotal passage. Timaeus has just finished describing the kinds of the various geometric molecules and their relationships with each other. The Platonic universe at 61c has two major elements: soul, both cosmic and human, and matter. Both types of soul are, at the very least, accidentally immortal. Plato now adds a third type of soul to his cosmology. He says that he must discuss the "ψυχῆς τε ὅσον θνητόν" (part of the soul that is mortal).

This is a remarkable promise. Plato intends to discuss a part of the soul that either dies or can die. This text demonstrates that Plato uses the term "ψυχή" (soul) to refer to a mortal element of the human creature. *Timaeus* is the only dialogue to make this distinction plain. It opens the possibility that soul may be used to refer to a mortal thing in other dialogues. One can not be sure in any dialogue that Plato means "immortal soul" when he uses the word "ψυχή" The *Symposium* contains a reference that might be an example of the alternative use of "ψυχή" to refer to "mortal soul." Diotima makes an important but passing reference to the "θνητὴ φύσις" in the *Symposium*, but her meaning is obscure.[114] In the *Timaeus,* this description comes up again and again. To cite another example in *Timaeus*, Plato uses "mortal soul" in his discussion of pleasures and pains. The pleasures and pains of the body are transmitted to the mortal soul.[115] This unprecedented and repeated use of terminology is highly significant to my thesis that the *Timaeus* contains the key description of the Platonic psychology.

What is this so significant? Plato has just finished describing the formation of the immortal soul. This immortal soul is usually taken to be the thing Plato is talking about when he uses the term ψυχή (soul) in other dialogues. In this passage, however, he makes it clear that another thing altogether, with different characteristics, merits his use of the term. Only in the *Timaeus* is this distinction made clear. While one can, perhaps, find hints of the distinction in other dialogues, it reaches its most mature state in the *Timaeus*. Yet the reader knows from his use of a similar term in passing in *Symposium*, that this sort of distinction is no innovation on the part of Plato late in life. The idea of a mortal soul may have been in his mind at least by the period in which the *Symposium* was written. It is, therefore, not a departure from his earlier thinking, but it is a unique and expansive clarification ot it.

The Mortal Soul: Creation and Function

The Location and Function of the Mortal Soul

What is the mortal soul that has appeared at different points in the unfolding of the Platonic psychology? The detailed answers to this complex question are saved for the last third of the dialogue. The reader is moving very close to full becoming and very far from the World of Being in examining the mortal soul. Plato has, therefore, saved it for the end of the dialogue.

At 69b, Plato recapitulates the description that he has given of the creation of the immortal soul. He reminds the reader that the god had created an immortal soul. The Father/Creator had turned this soul over to the demigods, his children.[116] Plato then says,

> They (the demigods) took over from him an immortal principal of the soul, and, imitating him, encased it in a mortal physical globe, with the body as a whole for vehicle. And they built on to it another mortal part, containing terrible and necessary feelings....[117]

Plato is now giving the reader his fullest account regarding the formation of the mortal part of the soul. Notice, however, that contrary to commentators like Cornford, this soul has been called by Plato a part of the whole soul. As Cornford acknowledges it must be the product of necessity, if the soul is to live in the world of Becoming. Since, however, creation of the immortal and mortal soul actually happen at the same instant, the mortal soul is an intrinsic part of what it is to be human. The mortal soul is second in words, but not in deed.

The soul is to become the seat of passions. These passions, both pleasures and pains, are described as morally negative. Pleasures are a "lure to evil." Pain puts "good to route."[118] "Irrational sensation" and "all daring lust" are blended with the passions to produce the mortal soul.

The lesser gods placed this part away from the immortal soul to avoid "polluting the divine element."[119] This part was placed by the demigods in the trunk area of the human and was connected to the divine soul through the neck. In this way, the immortal soul can communicate with the other part of the human soul without being overcome by its powerful passions. It comes into contact with less matter, due to the narrow "isthmus" of the neck.

The mortal soul was divided into two parts.[120] One part is deemed inferior to the other. The first, or superior, part of the mortal soul was the "seat of courage, passion, and ambition."[121] This part was chambered in the region of the human heart. The purpose of this component of the mortal soul was to act as a guard or guardian for the divine soul over the passions. Great care is taken by the gods, through such things as the provision of the lungs as emotional shock absorbers, to shield this portion from the terrible emotions of the lower part. As Taylor points out, this entire dividing process and the terminology employed is a direct and obvious link to the psychology of the *Republic*.[122]

The second part of the mortal soul was located near the navel. This part of the soul was the "appetite for food and drink and other natural needs."[123] It is the wild part of the soul and great care is taken by Plato to show that the demigods have placed it, as much as possible, under the control of the divine soul. The liver, for example, is placed there to act as a kind of constraining force for the rational soul.

It is necessary to the mortal soul and to the immortal soul to be separate, but also able to communicate. The mortal soul's main function is to connect the divine, immortal, and AS soul to the material world. How does this work? The passionate soul communicates the raw materials of creation to the chest. The chest in turn passes this information to the rational soul in the head. At each level, the data of the world of Becoming can be processed and tamed so that it does not destroy the harmony or purity of the rational soul. In this way, a filter system is created that allows the rational to come into contact with and, in some limited way, comprehend the irrational world of Becoming.

Plato created the immortal soul as a link between the World of Being and the world of Becoming. This immortal soul is still too divine to come into direct contact with becoming. The mortal soul occupies this middle ground between immortal soul and becoming.

The mortal soul is not, therefore, evil. It is a necessary part of the cosmic order. The relationship of the mortal soul to the immortal soul, though hinted at in the account at 43-47, was not spelled out. This could only be done after the introduction to the cosmology of Necessity at 48. The mortal soul and its works must be understood in this context and not with the neo-Platonic Christian notion of evil.

The passionate soul has no share of reason.[124] On the other hand, it is not designed to perform the reasoning function. It is no more to blame for its failure to reason than a wall is to blame for a like failure. It is only when the dreams and disorders of this part of the soul come to be taken seriously as reasonable that the soul gets into trouble. That is not their function. In some ways, the belly "intellectualizes" the confusing physical sensations with which it comes into contact. The problem with the mortal soul, therefore, is its tendency to dominate over the rational soul, not its existence. It is a necessary part of being a human. The mortal soul can communicate intellectual and spiritual information to the immortal soul through a complex process. This process is divination. It gives the immortal soul information that it could not otherwise receive.

Divination in the Mortal Soul

Divination is given to the belly as a gift of the gods. How can the belly region provide any knowledge to the immortal soul? Is this a mere jest on the part of Plato? What does this say about the relationship between the immortal and mortal regions of the soul?

Both Taylor[125] and Cornford [126] do not utterly dismiss this gift of divination as irony on the part of Plato. Both point out that divination did impart some shadowy knowledge to the soul. I agree with their conclusion on this point. Taylor and Cornford, however, picture the liver as speaking a sort of gibberish to the immortal soul. Out of this nonsense the immortal soul, somehow, gleans some knowledge. Taylor compares this process of divination in the human to the process of divination that took place at Delphi. He indirectly equates the role of the liver to that of the Pythia at Delphi.[127] Both commentators leave little role for the liver in helping shape the content of the oracle. I believe that Cornford and Taylor have placed too great a limitation on the role of the liver. This is caused by implicit notions about the workings of the Greek oracle on their part that are open to serious challenge.

The most popular oracle for the contemporary Athenian at the time of Plato, and the oracle about which modern scholars know the most, is the oracle at Delphi.[128] Regrettably, even in this best case, scholars still have much to learn about the various religious practices at Delphi. This is particularly the case in the role of the Pythia or the female member of the oracle presentation.

Traditionally the role of the Pythia has been seen as quite limited. The priestess received the oracle in some sort of drugged state and passed it on to the male prophet who made sense of it. Taylor compared the utterances of the Pythia to the New Testament practice of praying in unknown tongues.[129] In their seminal volume on Greek mythology, Morford and Lenardon say of the Pythia, "In a frenzy of inspiration she utters her incoherent ravings. A priest or prophet nearby will transcribe them into intelligible prose."[130] This is the traditional view.

If one views the Pythia's role in this manner, this will shape one's view of the role of the liver in divination. The Pythia is the "receiver" of the message from the gods at Delphi. The liver receives the oracle from the gods in the human body.[131] The Pythia performs the same function in Greek oracles, therefore, as the liver does in human divination. If the Pythia muttered mere "incoherent ravings," then it is no wonder both Taylor and Cornford downplay the role of the liver in imparting knowledge through divination.

This picture of Delphi can be challenged. We know that the priestess of Delphi could be bribed.[132] What would be the point of bribing someone who is merely mouthing meaningless gibberish? It would seem sensible to assume that the Pythia must have played a role in determining the content of the oracle. At the very least, she was believed to do so by the public. If this is not the case, then a bribe makes little sense. This taking of bribes is one of the few things we know for certain about the Pythia.

Walter Burkert concedes, "the exact oracular procedures followed cannot be determined precisely."[133] Given that fact, it seems best to assume that the Pythia transmitted at least part of the content of the oracle to the priest. The priest put the oracle received from her into poetic form. How much could the priest change the oracle he had received from the Pythia? We do not know. There is only one safe conclusion about the formation of the oracle: both the Pythia and the priest had some role to play.

If one accepts this more generous notion of the role of the Pythia, then one might grant an expanded role to the emotional soul than that allowed by Taylor and Cornford. Taylor and Cornford tend to see the voice of the liver as being irrational and doing little of the actual work of divination. The key role in any oracle was that of the priest in explaining the gibberish uttered by the female oracle. On my preferred interpretation, the Pythia was in control of a great deal of the content of the oracle. The prophet, therefore, confirmed and shaped the image, but he did not control the content. On the older account of the Oracle, the prophet controlled all three steps, with the female actor acting only as a sort of prop. If I am correct, then Plato would have assumed that his readers would have viewed the liver as an active player the reception of the content of the divination, not just a passive receiver of divine gibberish.

Suppose the divinity wishes to relay a message of doom to a supplicant. What will be the wording of that message? It appears that the form of the message depended on the wording and capabilities of the particular woman acting as Pythia. If one believes the oracle to be inspired, this is the only way to explain the different styles of the different utterances. This section of the *Timaeus* assumes that such divination is indeed possible.

If so, then reader of the *Timaeus* at the time of Plato might have assumed that the form of the message from the gods was under the control of the liver. In short, the reader would have compared his knowledge of the workings of the oracle to the Platonic picture describing divination. The belly would not just be receiving impressions that would then be passed on without change, and interpreted by the brain. The informed listener to Timaeus would know that the belly would play a critical role in shaping the form of the divine revelation. It would be up to the immortal or divine soul to confirm this sensible divine impression left on the belly and to give the revelation final shape in action. The immortal soul would, therefore, act in the role of both the prophet and the supplicant.

On this reading of the text, Plato has a way for the divine, either a god or the Forms, to correct the immortal soul. On the old reading, the role of divination must be treated as a sort of concession on the part of Plato to traditional piety. To the contrary, Plato has gained a new way of correcting the motions of the immortal soul. The divine soul, if confronted with a sensible divine message from the gods through the belly by means of divination, would be strengthened in its proper motions by pondering it. Astronomy, therefore, becomes a way to strengthen such motions from the top and divination is a way to do so from the bottom.

It might seem that the discussion at 71e would argue against my higher view of the role of the liver. A human who is rational, awake, or in his right mind does not divine. This passage attributes the pondering of the message of the liver to the immortal soul housed in the head of the body only after the madness or sleep of divination have passed. Does this argue for the old traditional view? I think not. The passage tells what it is the rational mind cannot do: divine or get the message from the gods.

This passage also limits how high a view of the role of the liver one can attribute to Plato. Certainly, Plato does not believe that the immortal soul of the head is going to be controlled by the liver or that the liver is going to directly issue rational commands to the body without the immortal soul being involved. The Pythia has her prophet.

Immortal soul is the sole possessor of reason. But the divine revelation transmitted from the gods by the liver, if it is not a meaningless bit of semantic garbage that can be bent in any way, will be a limitation to the immortal soul. The immortal soul that receives an oracle saying, "x is true," may stretch the meaning or the thrust of that oracle in very many directions, but not in unlimited directions. Oracles are open to many interpretations, but not to infinite interpretations. The gods' sensible messages transmitted from the liver will, therefore, limit or direct those areas to which the immortal soul, or mind, will pay attention. Dealing with revelation in this manner would not be unique to Plato. In fact, some modern philosophers of religion deal with sacred texts in a similar manner. They provide the raw and limiting data about what is viewed as true that the rational faculty then interprets.[134]

This reading is also sensible if Plato is an atheist. It could be that the ability to practice effective divination in a Platonic model is merely presented with the use of religious language. A more naturalistic read is possible. How? The liver is not involved in cognition itself. Plato makes the head, and the brain marrow in it, the sole seat of cognition. Cogitation is circular motion of the soul. The liver is not thinking, because it has no circular motion. It is, perhaps, aiding the brain area in restoring proper motion, but it is not itself participating in that motion. Minimally, for example, Plato is committed only to the special ability of the belly region, and the liver in particular, to transmit certain motions to the mind that would enable it to harmonize with the motions of the Same and the Different. The liver could be very receptive to the transmission of the influence of the Forms.

Of course, this is not an argument that the liver itself ever moves with these rational motions. To the contrary, if functioning properly, it is a transmitter of corrective motions to the immortal soul. To give a crude and simple example, if the immortal soul is moving with a circular motion that tilts right, the liver might relay an oracular impulse for motion to the left. This would tend to fix the motion of the immortal soul. The liver, of course, would be sharing in the motion to the right, not circular motion. The fact that Plato, in a traditional religious society, has couched such an interaction of Form and matter in religious or mythological language is not determinative on how to understand this passage.

According to the *Timaeus*, the rational mind acts as a prophet to interpret the divination for the people, in this case, the various parts of the body. For the most part, translators have worked with these passages in the *Timaeus* within the framework of the traditional understanding of Delphi. This has impacted their translation choices to make it appear that Plato supports the lower view of the female role at Delphi. The key passage follows: "Some persons call them prophets; they are quite unaware that they are only the expositors of dark sayings and visions, and are not to be called prophets at all, but only interpreters of prophecy."[135] This is the traditional translation as rendered by Benjamin Jowett. The two key mistranslations, if I am correct, are the use of "dark" and "interpreters" in the end of the text. The relevant Greek here are the terms "αἰνιγμῶν" and "δικαιότατα."

Jowett translates the first term as "dark saying." It is true that αἰνιγμῶν can be translated "dark saying." But what does it mean to say that the sayings are dark? Does it mean the traditional string of gibberish? If the word is examined further, then it appears that an αἰνιγμῶν is "a riddle" and not just a string of semantic rubbish. In other words, the Oracle provided the supplicant with a riddle that was hard to understand. This is in fact what one finds in examining the final products of the Oracle that have been preserved for modern readers. The "dark saying" was not something cleared up by the "prophet," but a riddle that helped the supplicant only if she or he could make sense of it. Understanding what the gods had said and trying to apply it to the situation was the job of the prophet.

What of the second term "δικαιότατα (prophet)?" The use of this term confirms my general theory about the role of women at Delphi. Plato uses δικαιότατα to name the prophets. The prophet is judging whether the Oracle is "righteous."[136] The prophet is not adding content to the riddle of the sibyl, but is merely stating whether the Sibyl has heard from the god. He may also act as a counselor in aiding the supplicant in applying the riddle to the life of the supplicant.[137]

This can directly apply to the psychology of the *Timaeus*. The rational mind does not create the divination, but seeks to apply it to the world scene. If one understands Plato as speaking metaphorically here about a physical process, then the immortal soul is using the divination that has passed through the liver to adjust the motions of the head region. Once again, this gives the reader the image of the belly or emotive region providing the raw data, in this case a divination, which the rational soul uses to encourage the making of sound judgements about the world of Becoming for the whole of the human.

If Plato is proposing divine revelation, he faces the problem of how the rational mind can be sure that any particular putative oracle is a working of the divine and not just indigestion. How does the brain know which of the states reported from the frenzy or the sleep by the liver are part of the oracle? Is it the case that the liver can only receive true and divine impressions? If it is, then the problem is solved; but the text is silent on the whole issue. Perhaps divine revelation is like many other things in the world of Becoming. It sometimes works, when it makes contact with the gods; sometimes it fails, when the liver has become disordered through the problems of living in the world of Becoming.

This allowance for divination is interesting in one other respect. If one takes it seriously, it reveals the status of the relationship between the rational human soul and the gods. The gods can speak to humanity, but only through the lowest part of humanity. Reason, human reason, is needed to apply the voice of the divine. Here is a picture of a human soul that is not subject to divinity, but merely uses the voice of divinity as an uncertain guide in an even less certain world. The human soul is autonomous. Religion and the revelations of religion do not stand in final judgement of the soul's actions. Indeed, the very existence of these divinities is shadowy and poorly described in the text. They seem to be, at most, personifications of the cosmic soul. They are no less created than the humans with whom they share the world of Becoming.

Problems for the Platonic Soul

Overview

By 72d, Plato has outlined the pattern for the shape of the soul. How does he view this account? He makes this clear by stating again that only God's signal of agreement could make one sure of its truth. It is, however, the most probable account. He affirms this positively. He says,

> Concerning the soul, then, what part of it is mortal, what part immortal, and where and with what companions and for what reasons these have been housed apart, only if God concurred could we dare to affirm that our account is true; but that our account is probable we must dare to affirm now, and to affirm still more positively as our inquiry proceeds: affirmed, therefore, let it be.[138]

In the Greek text the passage concludes: τὸ φάναι καὶ πεφάσθω. This is a very strong affirmation, as strong as it could be, without being certain truth. That sort of certainty is impossible of course in the world of Becoming, even about the soul.

The important details for the human psychology are in place. Plato has detailed the formation of an AS, rational, soul. This human soul, like the cosmic soul that is its model, is the rational element and the self-moving source of motion for its body. It has priority over all other things in the world of Becoming due to the appearance of a longer history, even if that appearance is not actual. It is, in the human being, always found in relationship with a lesser mortal soul. The immortal soul cannot itself be destroyed or fundamentally confused in its own nature as immortal soul, but can be overwhelmed in its interaction with the mortal soul and the cosmos. The mortal soul is not itself, however, utterly blind to the World of Being. It has, within the liver, the ability to communicate to the immortal soul the truth regarding the World. Most importantly, it serves as the middle ground between the immortal soul and the body. It contains some attributes of the immortal soul, such as invisibility, and some of the body, such as mortality.

There exists, however, at least three problems in this picture of the human soul that deserve attention. First, how does one individuate between human souls? This seems important to a robust concept of the immortality of a given human soul. Second, what is the status of the account of the creation of the human body? How sure can the reader be of the seriousness of this portion of the account? Finally, what is the appropriate relationship between animals and humans? If the proposed psychology is correct, what is the impact on the devolution proposed from humans to animals at *Timaeus* 90e?

The Problem of Individuation

The first problem for Plato, obvious at this point, is the ability within his psychology to individuate between immortal souls. It is true that the immortal soul of each individual human will live forever, but in what way is it unique from the any other soul? Is it the case that Socrates himself exists forever, as the *Phaedo* suggests, or does some self-moving bit of soul that once motivated Socrates just happen to continue? All soul motion has itself the same basic pattern; it has the same basic makeup. What makes my immortal soul different from that of Socrates?

First, it is of course possible to individuate between the soul of Plato, for example, and the soul of Socrates, on the basis of physical location. The soul of Socrates will never in all of its immortal history occupy the same space as the soul of Plato. For example, in the astral realm, when the soul is not incarnated, the soul of Plato and the soul of Socrates will exist on different stars. The reader of history knows, since Plato and Socrates were alive at the same time, that they did not share the same soul. Of course, this logically entails that the soul that moved Plato and the soul that moved Socrates were from different home stars. They may both be alive again at the same time, they may both be stars at the same time, but they are not the same motivating soul.

The soul of Socrates could therefore be individuated by simply saying of it that it is the "the soul that occupied star x, at a certain time t." In any scheme that includes reincarnation, of course, it will be impossible to differentiate between the souls of some people. In fact, if separated in time, they may share the same soul. In such cases, it would be correct to say that "Socrates" (if by Socrates we mean his immortal soul, the very essence of his being) is "Brenda" (if the soul of Brenda is from the same star as the soul of Socrates).

This is, of course, not what is meant in popular understandings of immortality. Humans think of "Socrates" as the man with the snub nose with certain characteristics that are products of the belly or the chest, like the love of argument. Humans hope for the survival of the mortal/immortal composite. They do not think of Socrates as only the rational faculty, housed on such and such a star, that directed the body and mortal soul of the man Socrates. Can the *Timaeus* provide for any survival of the composite?

On my reading it cannot, in any strong sense. This would not, I think, have troubled Plato as a philosopher. It might have been of little comfort to his friends at the time of the death of Socrates, but this would have only been a function of their weaknesses and irrationality. For Plato, that which was good in Socrates, the true and the reasonable, will live forever. The accidental features of Socrates, which may have made him lovable to the unwise, will perish. The lover of Socrates also need not fear that this immortal soul he has loved will just vanish as a drop in a broader cosmic pool of energy. The soul of Socrates has a unique place in the cosmos that will keep it forever apart from any other soul. Such person even has the hope of her soul meeting such a beloved soul in some future set of lives.

The wise human has always loved Socrates only for that part of his being that Plato has protected against death. The immortal soul, it must be recalled, is itself only accidentally immortal. It is a composite created by the Demiurge and could, in theory, be destroyed by Him. It is going to live forever, but this is not a necessary feature of its being. The unique reasoning soul that was in Socrates, for example, will survive. Plato has protected what he valued against any actual harm. He has done so only at the loss of what he believes he should not value or love, the accidental eccentricities of the man he knew.[139]

There is a sense where the mortal and immortal soul combination within Socrates might survive death or at least a few deaths. While not immortal over the course of infinite time, the mortal soul might continue for so long that it comes to look very much like immortality from the limited human perspective. Such a condition is not a desirable one within the Platonic cosmology, but it seems to exist. In the passages describing reincarnation of the immortal soul, Plato talks of features of the mortal soul clinging or being embedded in the immortal soul.[140] In the myths describing the judgment of the dead,   [141] souls return in the bodies appropriate to their nature. The soul of the wild human, for example, returns as a beast. I will defer for the moment the question of how this interaction works. It is enough to note that Socrates as a combination of the soul from a particular star and a mortal soul may survive, but that it would not be desirable. It is not something that would be wished by wise human beings at the death of a friend.

As I argued earlier, the soul stuff of Socrates needs to be fully fused through living the philosophic life. Failure to do this just might result in a stagnation at a certain level. Nevertheless, on the death of the average person, it might be accurate, in a rough way, for the philosopher to predict the survival of some part of the composite. The average human will not escape the endless cycle of incarnations, indeed it is not clear that Plato believes anyone has. It would always be a fair prediction to assume that some portion of the "personality" (the combination of the reasoning with the unreasoning souls) will survive to live again. Since the average person does not have his or her loves fixed on the right object,[142] it might comfort the average person to know that this beloved, viewed as an emotional being and not just as a reasoning force, is likely to survive death. It might even, in a very rough way, be possible to talk of such a combination as immortal since it is likely to continue for a very long time. Of course, in the *Phaedo*, these very notions are discussed. It is possible to view this discussion as a refinement of the views of the lovers of Socrates regarding the soul and immortality. In any case, the part of Socrates that is important to Plato does forever survive as an individual soul.

Status of the Account of the Creation of the Body

Plato describes the creation of the human body at 45-48 and again at 73-82. The details of this process are not, for the most part, of much help in fleshing out the psychology of the *Timaeus*. Later I will argue that the details are not accurate, because of the nature of the body or any other physical object in the world of Becoming. In what way, therefore, does this remaining portion of the dialogue make the account more probable? Plato is about to show that the cosmology and psychology he has taken such great pains to generate are going to be productive in explaining facts about the world of Becoming. Plato, in the language of modern philosophers of science, is going to demonstrate that his theory has both predictive and explanatory power. The ability of his point of view to both predict the shape of the natural world and to explain what happens in it will leave the reader confident of the probability of the theory.

Plato binds the mortal soul to the marrow of the bones.[143] Notice the clear physical connection Plato has made between the self-motion of the soul and the entire human body. Bone, of course, exists throughout the body. Marrow is the sap of the bones. It is a unique substance in which the soul is engendered, just as the marrow is contained within the bone. The marrow itself becomes the generative force of the body. It is formed of the very best and most pure geometric particles that can be found. It is blended in perfect proportion. It is the closest thing to a divine substance that can be made in the visible world.

Soul, as the life force, is captured within the fine and perfectly mixed marrow (The marrow that holds the immortal soul is called "brain." The brain, like the universe, is perfectly spherical according to Plato). The marrow is anchored to the spine and the other bones of the body.[144] The mortal and immortal soul act on the marrow/brain. The marrow/brain acts on the body. This whole dynamic structure is referred to by Plato as the "πάσης ψυχῆς."[145] This all -encompassing soul-system allows the human to theoretically function in the world of Becoming while retaining knowledge of the World of Being. A bridge between the two radically disparate elements of Plato's metaphysics has been created in the Form of the human soul.

The just city, as Plato used it in the *Republic*, was an image that enabled him to picture the just soul. It was the desire for this sort of clear vision that drove the discussion of the early *Republic*.[146] The *Timaeus* has allowed the same sort of clarity, by once again moving from the great to the small. Just as this vision of the most just city allowed the reader to better see the just human, so the vision of the most probable cosmic order has allowed the reader to catch a glimmer of the most probable psychological order in humankind. Socrates, as he requested at the start of the dialogue,[147] is being given, in a feast of words, a description of what his hypothetical city and soul would have looked like in the actual world.

The rest of the body is created to protect and serve the soul-system. Flesh, for example, allows the soul to be protected in hard falls. The entire creation of the human frame is teleological. Things are created to work as well as they can, given the demands of Necessity. To cite just one minor example, as little flesh as possible is placed on the joints to preserve flexibility. Protection and agility are kept in the best possible balance for the proper functioning of the human soul. As Plato sadly notes at 75c, the "δημιουργοῖς" (craftsman, maker) of the human body could not create a safe and long-lived animal and a rational or good animal. The human frame is designed to maximize intelligence, not safety.

This has an important, practical consequence for the human soul-system. In seeing what this consequence is, it will be vital to more clearly see the relationship between the marrow of the body and the soul. This, coupled with the knowledge that the human frame is designed for reasoning and not for durability, will explain the large numbers of non-human creatures in the world. Humans are frail, and this frailty leads to the abundance of non-human living things.

Why is this so? The human being is the product of the relationship between the soul-system and the body. The soul-system itself is the product of a further union of mortal and immortal souls.

The soul-system is quite likely to be destroyed before it has a chance to adjust to its new relationships.

At the conception of at least some humans, a fresh immortal soul is placed in relationship with a mortal soul and with a body. The new immortal soul is initially overwhelmed by such contact. It will take time for the soul to right the relationship and establish proper order in the new composite. As has already been discussed, however, this soul can become utterly entangled and confused in this relationship so that it cannot escape. What does that mean? Is there a more naturalistic way to understand Plato's mythical and religious language in the light of the soul-system's physical functions?

I believe that such a natural account is possible, and is suggested by this section of the text seen in the light of what has come before it. The soul and the marrow are in constant communication with the rest of the soul composite and the body. The brain serves as the operating medium for the motion of the immortal soul. In an ideal human soul composite, or at least in a mature human soul composite, the marrow would be fully directed by the proper response to the motion of the soul. The brain marrow would be moving, constantly, in the motion of the same. It is important to note in light of earlier discussions that marrow is made from the finest materials in the cosmos. It is the easiest to move.[148]

But what of the human being that is not in such a state? This would presumably include all infant humans and most adults, since most adults are clearly not cultivating the ordering of the motions of their bodies through the proper disciplines. Such humans, most of the race, would possess an immortal soul still in the contact stage of ordering the brain marrow. Their brain marrow would not yet have achieved full integration with the motion of the immortal soul. The soul of a human of this sort would still be attempting the proper union and motion with the marrow at the moment of death. It would, therefore, necessarily, still be in full contact with the brain marrow.

This would not be the case in the ideal human. A fully mature human, with a brain in proper motion, would only need to right the motion of his brain on certain occasions should it be disturbed by an outside force. This would make the soul of this mature human able to return to its star unencumbered. The need for a comparatively weak human frame, however, means that many humans will never even have a chance to get to such a state, before they are caught in death. Their souls will be thrown from their bodies while still in the process of directing the initial ordering of the motion of the brain.

At *Timaeus* 90b, Plato describes the soul as reaching immortality by making strong the rational part of the soul. He turns at 90b-91 to the punishments that await the person who feeds the mortal parts of his soul. This human runs the risk of being born a second time as a woman or some type of animal. It is not clear, however, whether Plato intends the language at 90-91, describing the death of humans, to be taken literally or figuratively. This brings the reader to the question of the relationship of the soul to matter or irrational motion at the moment of death.

The Soul at the Moment of Death

Can soul be entangled in matter? Can distortion in its proper motion linger after death? If the soul is able to remain warped or entangled with the mortal portions after death,[149] as the direct language of the *Timaeus* 89-91 implies, then this would give an easy physical explanation for the immediate reincarnation of such warped souls in animals. One need not worry that such a soul would be in any danger of being destroyed. If it is entangled in a composite that survives death, then it would simply, "like to like," move to an appropriate body. If that composite came apart, then it would cleave first on the line of the matter and the soul. Such a fortunate and free soul would then be AS[150] and could not be destroyed. It would return to its star.

On the other hand, if the language is figurative and no matter can cling to the soul or warp its motions after death, the soul is free to return to the star. The process of reincarnation could be explained on other grounds. Divinity in the cosmos could judge such a soul for its bad life and return it for further purifications. On a more physical account, it might be returned for further purification of its soul substance as I suggested when discussing the creation of the human soul by the God. A bad life would, therefore, have cut short the necessary purification of the soul. It would have to be returned to continue the process.

Plato says of the soul,

> Whoso, then, indulges in lusts or in contentions and devote himself overmuch thereto must of necessity be filled with opinions that are wholly mortal, and altogether, so far as it is possible to become mortal, fall not short of this (mortality) in even a small degree, inasmuch, as he has made great his mortal part.[151]

This certainly seems to imply that the evil done to the soul continues after death. The context of the passage is the discussion of the sickness of the body and the soul and their cure that begins at 87c. What is the way to health? *Timaeus* 90d says, "… supply each part of the soul with its own congenial food and motion…." This is important, because the passage sums up Plato's opinion about the result of this sickness in the world of Becoming on the human.

I believe the text supports the idea that, at least, distortion of motion can continue for a time after death. The soul does not right itself immediately. The revolutions of the human head, the brain marrow and the soul in union are disturbed, and need to be righted. How can this be done? How do humans know what is the right motion or proper food?

The proper motion is potentially there all the time. The soul never loses its basic nature, even if it is suppressed in a particular combination. It is there to be restored, if we give it the proper medium, or marrow, to use by feeding ourselves correctly. This feeding, of course, includes ingesting the proper physical components to make up the marrow and the proper intellectual intake to maximize the tendency to receive motion proper to the brain marrow when it comes into contact with the soul. The soul is, thereby, placed in a more congenial environment. Its natural rational motion is thus allowed to dominate.

What happens to the soul where this feeding is neglected? There is a way to understand how such neglect could hurt the soul even if matter could not cling to it. It might remain, even if for only a moment, in its irrational motion. Let me expand on my earlier suggestions. Such a soul at the moment of death of an immature person would be fully engaged in improper motion with his or her brain matter. What is that brain matter like? It could be different in each person. A person who has indulged his lusts may have built a dense and cumbersome bit of marrow in his brain. The soul would, therefore, not be engaged in the pure motion of the Same with the brain marrow at the moment of death. Only pure brain marrow in an ordered body could allow such a motion. The mixed and cumbersome marrow of the ill-fed or immature human would move with a mixed motion appropriate to it; the motion of the Same would be mixed with some of the motions appropriate to water or earth, for example.

Such an unfortunate soul would, at the point of death, be thrown instantly to its star and be in an improper relationship to it. Its motion would wrong, even if no matter from the marrow still clung to it. Of course, if the marrow came with the soul to the star the problems would be even worse. The matter would long to fall back to its like substance below. In either case, the soul of such a human would be in a difficult position. What would be the result ? This soul would find itself applying the inappropriate motion within the astral plane. It would be in conflict with the motion of the cosmic soul. Such a soul would be expelled back to a level with matter appropriate to its disposition at the moment of death.

By contrast, the soul of the healthy human, at the death of the body, would go from the rotations of the brain marrow in the circle of the Same to the rotations of the stars in the same motion. It would, in this ideal situation, be able to stay on the star as its initial motion would be in exact agreement with that being given to the star by the cosmic soul. My account could be summarized in the following manner:

1. The immortal human soul will, when mixed with a body, move with the best possible motion (i.e., the one most like circular motion).
2. Some bodies and impulses to motions that they contain can prevent this possible motion from being the proper motion of the soul.
3. Such difficult bodies will, therefore, receive improper motions.
4. A human soul in the astral plane moves with its star and the cosmic soul in the motion of the Same.
5. The ability of the cosmic soul to move a star is greater than the ability of the human soul to do so.
6. Given the truth of 5, human soul that attempts, because of a premature or unfortunate death, to move his or her star improperly will be unable to do so.
7. Such a human soul complex will find a body in the cosmos appropriate to its motion in "like being drawn to like."

Plato has, therefore, a consistent account of motion and the soul available to him. This account also gives a natural explanation for the repeated incarnations of the human. Plato has made it clear that human body confuses the newly incarnate soul.[152] Getting the proper motion restored to the soul depends on education, moral behavior, body type, and the politics of the city in which one lives.[153] These facts, taken in conjunction with the nature of the soul, provide a purpose for a fact about the natural world.

There exists more soul, in a non-technical sense, in the world in non-humans than in humans. In other words, there are more non-human animals than human animals. Did Plato realize this? It is unclear, but seems likely. This, however, would have been exactly what he would have expected given his view of the soul and the nature of the human frame. Most souls, sown in human frame, would be by chance alone thrown back to their stars in an unfit state. This would lead, as deeper analysis has shown, to a natural increase in non-human animated bodies. In the end, it is amazing that humans continue at all, rather than that there are so few of them.

What of the good or proper soul? Does it forever escape the bondage of incarnation in non-astral bodies? This is not clear. The *Timaeus* says nothing directly on the issue. I have a suggestion to make based on an idea gleaned from *Republic*. Passages in the *Republic*, especially at the end of Book VII and Book X, lead me to believe that it cannot escape. In book VII of the *Republic,* the philosopher must, in justice, return to the city-state and aid the people there. In Book X,[154] the myth describes even the best souls returning to human life. I believe the *Timaeus* provides a cosmological justification for this hard duty of the good man.

The cosmos is under the rule of both Reason and Necessity. Reason is not omnipotent for it must work within the constraints of Necessity. The world of Becoming is between the World of Being and the nothingness of non-being. As such, all souls act as a stabilizing cosmological principle. The world within the υ'ποδοχή (space) is an unstable world. Necessity is constantly driving it toward chaos. On the other hand, cosmic soul regulates the contrary motions of the astral sphere and brings order and restraint to the potential disorder. The human soul, on my view, performs the same function in the body. It may, therefore, be just in the sense of appropriate for the soul to return to the earth for this purpose. This might be true even of a very good man. It is, therefore, at least appropriate for the human soul to carry the divine order that it has seen in the astral relationship to the more confused sub-lunar area of becoming. This is, of course, only a suggested solution. The *Timaeus* itself could be read either way.

Plato's vision of the details of the construction of the human body meshes nicely with a naturalistic and consistent version of his psychology. Of course, I have also allowed for a mythical or religious understanding of much of the text. The psychology presented so far is flexible on this difficult point. Plato's psychology is coming together with his cosmology in a unified whole.

Plato's Views on "Science" Relation to His Psychology

One should remember that the truth or falsity of the particular postulated mechanisms of the soul in the world of Becoming is not important to Plato. If my earlier claims were correct, and Plato is committed to his psychology, then it is vital to see the particular physical models as demonstrations of that psychology in the world of Becoming. The lungs may not work like giant lobster traps, as Plato pictures them, but Plato has still given the reader an image of a soul and body functioning in a harmonious soul-system. Plato was, of course, skeptical that any theory regarding the world of Becoming would be true or enduring. He could have picked what moderns would view as the right description of the lung system and circulation and it would have been consistent with his psychology.

Of course, I am not claiming that any change in his conception of the physical universe would have not disturbed his psychology. In fact, the opposite is true. Plato's psychology had implications in the natural world, as we have seen. Plato's psychology postulates unity amongst living things. If that unity does not exist, then his psychology would be undermined. If the major motivation for the hypothesis of the soul, explaining motion, is better dealt with in other ways, then Plato's view of the soul is at least made very improbable.

In the modern world of relativity theory, for example, one may no longer feel the need for the notion of soul to provide for motion or the potential for motion. I am not arguing, therefore, that Plato was right in his psychology or that all his errors are unimportant, but that each error of detail in his descriptions of physiological systems do not by themselves falsify the general psychology. Plato could be committed to the one without a full commitment to details of the other. He needs a certain type of cosmology, not a specific cosmology. I will have more to say about the implications of this feature of the psychology later.

The existence of other living beings in the world of Becoming is something that is going to be a natural consequence of the psychology and physiology of adult males. Plato notes at 76e that both women and living animals come from men. To understand the psychological and physical structure of man is, therefore, to understand these structures in all living animals. Man contains in one form or another every feature that the animals who will spring from him will need. His nails; for example, serve as prototypes for the laws that are to come on man's "children." Man is the parent of all sorts of living animals. They devolve from him as he fails to live up to the rational lifestyle demanded of him by his place in the cosmic order.

What are the consequences of these scientific ideas for Plato's psychology? First, Plato has unified all life into one sort of thing. Life in the world of Bcoming is that which is moved as a result of contact with human soul. Second, his picture of the devolution of the soul also provides an explanation, and not just a myth or just-so-story, for the origin of the species. This delivers Plato from an important modern attack on his cosmological views. He is often described as giving a theory that explains too much and thus explains nothing.

Karl Popper, in setting up his own philosophy of science, describes Plato as providing, in contrast to his own view, "a theory of ultimate explanation; that is to say of an explanation whose explicans is neither capable nor in need of further explanation."[155] Plato's cosmology is a dead end for the modern researcher or the student of nature. Popper says Platonism can be accepted in its totality, but it cannot be the seedbed for a fruitful research program. If this way of reading of Plato is correct, Plato's cosmology and psychology have more in common with certain contemporary religious ways of looking at the cosmos than with the best contemporary science.

Does Plato's psychology make science impossible? Let me state some important limitations to my attempt to answer this question. First, I shall not discuss issues within philosophy of science in any great detail or the demarcation of questions regarding science and non-science. I am merely examining a few of the implications of Plato's psychology for the study of the natural world. Second, it is not my intention to attribute a full philosophy of science to Plato. I am not even sure that such a project would be possible.

Plato's views in his psychology would have important implications for a Platonic philosophy of science. It is this fact which will deliver Plato from the charge often leveled against him, that he leaves the scientist out of work. Contrary to Popper, a correct reading of Plato's cosmology leads to a potential research program for Platonic scientists. To lapse into Popper's jargon, Plato's view is falsifiable after a fashion. For Plato, of course, a cosmological theory is not true or false, strictly speaking. In Plato's language, his cosmology could be rendered improbable or, conversely, probable by examination. Plato does not, of course, develop a scientific theory in the modern sense. It is not, on the other hand, an unfruitful program of merely "mythical" status.

How has Plato's psychology helped avoid this trap? Plato has pictured human soul as being the motive force behind and the cause of other living things. The dog by the fire simply is a human soul in a profoundly degraded condition. The human animal is, on Plato's view as it has been developed, necessarily the first living creature in the world of Becoming.[156] Humans and animals should share many basic features in common. It should be possible to develop a hierarchy of animals based on the physical nature of the matter making up the ideal brain marrow of the animal. Matter that is very dense or mixed with great amounts of earth or water should be found in the brain marrow of lower animals. If the brain marrow of lower animals should turn out to be physically identical with that of humankind, this would force a radical reworking of the Platonic psychology.

Plato has made, therefore, certain predictions about the world while developing his psychology. These are predictions that follow so closely on the theory that he must take them seriously. Once again, this is not to suggest that he must take all the more remote speculations seriously. For example, it is not necessary for Plato that the elements be exactly the four postulated in traditional Greek science. His theory could be reworked to include new elements. There are some parts of the cosmology more certain than others, based on their proximity to the Platonic psychology. Plato's science matters.

Does this contradict the basic Platonic doctrine that a science of the world of Becoming is impossible? It does not. As was shown in examining the opening portions of the dialogue, Plato could not and did not believe humans could have strong and sure knowledge about the world of Becoming, but they could have accounts about that world that were more or less probable. A Platonist does not have to despair of being able to ever choose between two competing ways of looking at the functions of the cosmos. She chooses neither solely on the basis of the facts of the empirical world, which for her do not exist, or on the basis of a whimsical subjectivism. A Platonist can choose the most probable story available based on his or her metaphysical views. She can also be aware of the fact that if her metaphysical views, ideas based of putative knowledge from the World of Being, are true, then the appearances of the world of Becoming should take a certain form in most places and at most times. In other words, Platonism makes certain predictions, in even its most rarified form, about the cosmic structure.

To cite but one example, a Platonist would expect from her psychology and the cosmology generated from it that theories about the cosmos would always be underdetermined. She would never anticipate that scientific theories would gain an equal, or even roughly equal, epistemological status with the knowledge gained from an acquaintance with the Forms. The Platonist is able to at least make negative predictions about the status of knowledge in the world of Becoming. These predictions are potentially open to falsification.

I have, however, complicated this simple cosmological picture even further. I have suggested that the human soul-system operates for Plato in a median position between the two worlds. It clearly functions in the world of Becoming, but it has many of the attributes that allow for knowledge when found in the World of Being. The soul, as Plato says in *Phaedo*, is most like the Forms. By its very nature, however, it will impact the world of Becoming in an intimate way. Of course, since this world is becoming, it can only impact the shape of the on-going gestation and not a final product. The soul would, however, limit the appearance of certain portions of the world of Becoming during this process. The soul is always actualizing motions, and hence is itself always a becoming thing, but these becomings are rational. They are, as a result, predictable.[157]

A consistent failure for the world of Becoming to conform in these basic ways would call the psychology into question. We must recall that even Plato, though very sure indeed about the psychology, has allowed that only Divine help would make this knowledge sure.[158] Divine help seems unavailable. The psychology of Plato, therefore, occupies an interesting epistemological ground. It is very close to the sure knowledge that humans gain from the World of Being, but it is not quite there. It is, after all, possible that Plato has gotten cosmology and psychology wrong. How would he ever know this has happened? I believe it is because investigation of the appearances of the physical world could make certain key features of his psychology much less probable.

Popper and critics to the contrary, Plato's psychology has actually been rendered much less probable with the passage of time. Plato encouraged at least some scientific observation, and that very observation has tended to undermined the plausibility of his view. For example, it is simply not the case that astronomical phenomenon of any sort are eternal or even close to eternal. This is an important blow to Plato's psychology. It does not make the psychology false for Plato; science could never do that. It does, however, decrease the firmness of our belief in that psychology. I will now to turn to an important case of the interaction of the psychology with theorizing about the biological world.

Animals and the Human

One area where Plato's psychology determines his views on the natural world is zoology. Human soul is not unique to incarnate human animals. Other animals, for example, have human souls in a complex soul-system. Since it is the divine, immortal soul that is the fundamental attribute of importance, humans are like animals in the most important and basic ways. It should also be noted that humans and animals share the lower soulish impulses of the chest and the belly region. As Plato points out in *Republic,* when he refers to his ideal guardians as whelps or dogs, the animal kingdom shares with humans the chest impulses, including higher examples like courage.[159] Animals are often described as the paradigm case of those things that have the erotic impulse.[160]

What does this mean? It means that for Plato, more than any other ancient or most modern thinkers, there was no substantial difference between animals and humans. Humans were those beings in which soul could best manifest its nature and proper relationship with the cosmos. They were, however, fundamentally like the lower animals around them in terms of their composition. A human uninterested in philosophy, or the arts, or astronomy should not be distinguishable from a beast in some important ways. This makes the reader take a great deal of Platonic imagery more seriously.

When Thrasymachus acts like a "beast" in his interjection in *Republic* Book I, there is more than symbolism at work. Thrasymachus, who has rejected the life of the mind has, for Plato, become a beast in every important respect. The fact that he is not usually perceived as such by his fellow creatures is due only to their confusion between the importance of the shell of his bodily form and where he is heading. Most humans are, therefore, not superior to animals in any way. This should have many ethical implications for Plato, though it is not clear that he cashed these out clearly. For example, should it be ethical to eat meat, if one accepts a Platonic psychology?[161]

There are at least two different ways Plato might have responded to such a question. First, he could have argued that eating the flesh of animals was wicked, because they contain human souls. Meat eating would be murder. Second, Plato could have argued that killing animals sets free a human soul in intolerable bondage. The second suggestion is rendered highly implausible by the ethics

propounded by Socrates in *Phaedo*. If it is not ethical to free humans
held in bondage to human bodies by killing them or for humans to
commit suicide, then why would it be ethical to "free" humans bound
in animal bodies? The dead animal has a soul that is, in all probability,
least likely to be ready for a journey to the astral realm. I believe that,
consistent with the first suggestion and my general picture of the
Platonic psychology, there is, therefore, much in Plato to favor
vegetarianism.

There are two texts that strongly suggest this to the careful
reader, if we conjoin to them our knowledge of basic Platonic thought.
I think the *Laws* presents such a principle. The text in *Laws* 798a says,

> Thus, if one were to look at bodies, one would see how they become
> accustomed to all foods and all drinks even if at first they were upset
> by them; one could see how, with the passage of time, they grow, out
> of these very materials, flesh that is akin to these things, and come to
> like, be accustomed to and familiar with, a whole regimen—thriving
> on in the best way from the point of view of both pleasure and
> wealth.[162]

What general and applicable principle can be derived from this
passage? Plato believes that a person becomes what they eat! If one
combines this with the earlier notion, that certain sorts of matter,
motions associated with matter, or amounts of matter are harmful to the
proper function of soul, then it is clear that one needs to exercise care in
the what one eats. This is consistent with the discussion of health and
eating that comes later in the *Timaeus,* where health is associated with a
proper diet. The soul of such a person has "incontinence in pleasure."[163]
Such a human is made impotent by the indulgences of erotic impulses.
In the *Laws*, Plato makes it clear that the impulse to eat is included in
his list of erotic impulses. In fact, it takes first place amongst them.[164]

Given both of these doctrines; that humans become what they
eat[165] and that the soul can be hindered by the physical substance[166]
with which it comes into contact; it would be unwise for humans to eat
meat. First, they would be killing another soul. Humans should not kill
other humans, since it is not their place in the cosmic order to make
such decisions. Socrates implicitly makes an argument like this in the
Phaedo when he is discussing suicide.[167] Animals simply are human
souls connected to a different physical being.

This sheds light on a second passage in *Laws*. Plato often
describes the ideal time as being in a Golden Age in the past. He does
this in Atlantis legend in both *Timaeus* and the unfinished *Critias*. In

Laws 732b he says,

> In fact, we see that even now the practice of human beings sacrificing
> one another still persists among many peoples. And we hear just the
> opposite about other peoples: how there was once a time when we did
> not dare to taste cattle, and sacrificed to the gods no animals, but
> instead gruel and fruits soaked in honey and other such hallowed
> sacrifices. They abstained from flesh on the grounds that it wasn't
> pious to eat it or pollute the altars of the gods with blood. Those of us
> who existed then had ways of life that were what is called "Orphic":
> we partook of everything that lacked soul but abstained from the
> opposite, from everything that possessed of soul.[168]

Pangle, in his interpretive essay,[169] sees this passage as describing two
extremes. He believes Plato[170] would condemn both the humans who
sacrificed each other and the humans who would not eat animals.

In the light of what has been learned about the psychology of
the *Timaeus*, is that at all a plausible reading of the text? Does it not, in
fact, do an injustice to the language of the text itself?[171] Plato has first
spoken of a group of people coming from the past, but who still exist in
the modern world. These people are engaged in human sacrifice. On the
other hand, humans who will not sacrifice any living animal are
described in positive terms. Why this high regard for animal life?
Animals have human souls. Such extinct humans lived Orphic lives.
This is another favorable comment. Plato is comparing one bad group
to a second good group. The cult of the present city does not look good
by comparison to the latter. It is not, after all, the purpose of the *Laws*
to defend the status quo, but to attempt to build a more just polis.
Plato's psychology within *Timaeus* has a direct and practical impact
both on the reading of a difficult text and on the ethical lives of the
ideal human. I contend that this ideal Platonic human would have been
vegetarian.

There is a problem with this argument for vegetarianism in
Plato, however. If Plato felt that "you are what you eat," then isn't it
better to eat higher life forms? Plants, after all, are even lower on the
scale of life than animals. Why eat them and become potentially
enmeshed in their lower souls and bodies?

There are two things that should be said before attempting to
resolve this issue. First, I have already pointed out that for Plato eating
itself, as an enterprise of the erotic nature, should be minimized. One
should not stop eating animals to indulge in the overeating of plants.
Second, Plato handles the formation of plants and animals in very

different ways within the *Timaeus*. It is important to note that plants are the final type of living being created. Their creation is explicitly for our nutritional benefit. Plato says, "And when our superiors had generated all these kinds (referring to the plants) as nutriment for us inferior beings...."[172] The same is never said of animals.

Animals come into being through human failure, and contain human soul as a matter of their very existence. Plants, on the other hand, are created with a kind of soul, but they have only the "third kind of soul, the belly soul."[173] Plants possess sensation and desires. They are, however, mortal and fail to reason and do not have even the bare potential to reason. There is no evidence to suggest that immortal soul ever comes to live in a plant. There are, therefore, textual and ontological differences between plants and animals in Plato. Ethically, plants can be eaten, because they do not contain a rational soul, even potentially. Humans and other animals cannot be eaten because they do.

Plato felt that humans were not in a position to take the life of an ensouled being. That does not mean, however, that eating vegetables is good for a human. Has Plato created a cosmology where humans must do something that is bad for them in order to be ethical? In other words, humanity would be better off eating humans and other animals, but the gods have forbidden it. In a world that is designed and has purpose, this seems an unlikely turn of events.

It is important to step back and examine the medical context out of which Plato operated. For this, I will turn to the writings of the founder of medicine, who lived at the same time as Plato. It is not important to my argument that Plato be familiar with the arguments of Hippocrates himself, just that those writings reflect the opinions of the established medical community just prior to the time of Plato's writing his final works. Hippocrates, in *On Ancient Medicine,* said:

> But to go still further back, I hold that the diet and food which people in health now use would not have been discovered, provided it had suited with man to eat and drink in like manner as the ox, the horse, and all other animals, except man, do of the productions of the earth, such as fruits, weeds, and grass; for from such things these animals grow, live free of disease, and require no other kind of food. And, at first, I am of opinion that man used the same sort of food, and that the present articles of diet had been discovered and invented only after a long lapse of time, for when they suffered much and severely from strong and brutish diet, swallowing things which were raw, unmixed,

and possessing great strength, they became exposed to strong pains and diseases, and to early deaths. It is likely, indeed, that from habit they would suffer less from these things then than we would now, but still they would suffer severely even then; and it is likely that the greater number, and those who had weaker constitutions, would all perish; whereas the stronger would hold out for a longer time, as even nowadays some, in consequence of using strong articles of food, get off with little trouble, but others with much pain and suffering. From this necessity it appears to me that they would search out the food befitting their nature, and thus discover that which we now use: and that from wheat, by macerating it, stripping it of its hull, grinding it all down, sifting, toasting, and baking it, they formed bread; and from barley they formed cake (maza), performing many operations in regard to it; they boiled, they roasted, they mixed, they diluted those things which are strong and of intense qualities with weaker things, fashioning them to the nature and powers of man, and considering that the stronger things Nature would not be able to manage if administered, and that from such things pains, diseases, and death would arise, but such as Nature could manage, that from them food, growth, and health, would arise. To such a discovery and investigation what more suitable name could one give than that of Medicine? since it was discovered for the health of man, for his nourishment and safety, as a substitute for that kind of diet by which pains, diseases, and deaths were occasioned.[174]

This is a complicated passage, but one can derive two relevant facts from it. Some important members of the medical community at the time of Plato did not feel that it was prudent to eat "strong" or raw foods like beasts. This portion of the medical community, including the prominent Hippocrates, did believe it better or safer to eat prepared or processed foods. These two facts do much to explain why Plato would have found it better, apart from his ethical grounds, to have plants as the basic material consumed by humans. First, meat was not normally eaten in a highly processed manner in the ancient world. To process food is to "reason" with it. A human adds information.

Vegetable materials, like wheat in bread, were often processed. Plato could well have thought that the process of preparing the vegetable matter simplified the potential for contrary motion of the lower matter. It might have appeared better to eat processed lower vegetable matter, than to eat unprocessed animal meat. Plant products were the staples of a simple life. Meat was not widely available in this period and was a bit of a luxury. In eating the common, prepared vegetables, one would not be eating the body itself or the Form. The meat-eater would be eating that body. Plato could, therefore, argue that one should not, on practical grounds, eat unprepared or simpler vegetable dishes. Prepared vegetables dishes were the weakest living matter that one could consume. The simple bodies of plants were reconstituted in such a way to impart the sustenance to the body without passing on much of the low elements or their motions.

It should also be remembered that a plant body was not designed to restrain the motions of the powerful soul. Its existence is gross, but at the same time, it is in some ways weaker and therefore easier to destroy and use. No human soul ever exists in a plant body for Plato; perhaps plants are not strong enough to receive such souls. Plant matter broken up and cooked would be in no position to defy or attempt to contain the motions of the immortal soul. The erotic impulses, which plants share, are often described as powerful, but that should not confuse the reader as to their real nature. The erotic impulse is potentially the weakest of the soul's motions. It gains strength only from the grossness of the surroundings. It appears to be strong, and indeed is strong, only in the world of Becoming. The soul as soul is potentially much more powerful, if it can control its contact with the grosser elements of the world of Becoming.

Finally, the preparing of vegetable food, to a far greater extent than the ancient preparation of animal meat, was an art. Raising animals might have been an art, in the case of the shepherd, but killing one required little skill. It is the shepherd who is admired by Plato, not the butcher. The baker and the wine-maker were highly esteemed members of the Greek community. These were skilled professionals. The baker and the wine-maker both added their skill to the raw wheat or grapes. In some sense, therefore, both wine and bread were the products of intelligence. This was true to a much lesser degree of the leg of mutton hanging over the fire on a spit. Intelligence has shaped the vegetable matter and, to some extent, tamed it. It remains a potentially disabling substance still, but one that can also do good. No such case can be made for animal products in the ancient world.

Plato has, therefore, developed his full psychological account by the end of 89. He will provide more details to that account in the concluding portions of the *Timaeus*, but the framework will remain the same. For a human, the moments of sickness, when the immortal and mortal souls are disturbed, and death, when the soul is set free, are times for careful psychological observation. Plato's reflections on the cause of these two twin phenomena, sickness and death, will make clear his unique brand of psychological dualism.

Psychological Dualism

Introduction to the Issues

Plato has been described as a dualist.[175] What is meant by this statement? A person is a dualist in a given situation, if, when answering a question about the nature of a thing or process, she theorizes that the thing or process has exactly two parts and that neither part can be reduced to the other. One can be a dualist in one area of study, without being a dualist in every area. For example, one could be a dualist about a process within human beings, without being a substance dualist. It has been claimed by some philosophers that Plato was a dualist in both his view of reality and in his psychology. Frank Thilly says of Plato's description of the things that exist, "If we had to label this part of the system, we should call it dualism: the idea is the paramount principle of things, and matter an inferior and secondary principle; but neither is reducible to the other."[176] Thilly describes Plato's psychology in the following manner, "Plato's psychology is dualistic in its separation of the soul into a higher rational, and a lower, irrational part...."

What do the cosmology and the psychology found in the *Timaeus* reveal about such claims? Based on my reading of *Timaeus*, I do not believe Plato was a substance dualist. My second challenge will be to show that Plato is, at least in one sense, a dualist in his description of human beings. For Plato, humans consist of both souls and bodies. Soul and body cannot be reduced to each other in terms of their interactions with each other. On the other hand, both soul and body are the same sort of thing, a becoming thing. Plato is not a dualist as to the substance of humans. This weak dualism will not leave Plato open to the standard objection to psychological dualism. The objection hinges on problems in the interaction of soul and body. I will show that the weak-Form Platonic dualism escapes this criticism.

Plato and Substance Dualism

Plato is not a substance dualist. I have already argued Plato believes in only one real type of substance: the Forms of the world of Becoming.[177] It could be maintained that these Forms   themselves are simply human ways of talking about Form Itself.[178] Everything within the cosmos is not real in the strong sense of the term. Everything, including soul, is in a position that is between full is and is not. Those

things that are coming into being draw whatever similarities they have
to being from the Forms. I will later argue that Plato does believe
humans, as part of the world of Becoming, have two parts. Plato is a
dualist in terms of what he believes about humanity. Humans have both
bodies and souls. This does not make him a substance dualist. As part
of the world of Becoming, humans are not, strictly speaking, real.

Plato allows only one reality: the World of Being. For Plato,
there exists an intermediate state between this one reality and
nonexistence, that he calls the world of Becoming.[179] The soul is a part
of this world of Becoming. It cannot, therefore, be described as an "is"
but it is also not an "is not." The soul is not a spirit in the traditional
Christian or Cartesian sense of a thing outside the cosmos that comes to
inhabit a body. It is not a substance. In terms of substance, Plato is not
a dualist.

The World of Becoming: the Nature of Soul and Matter

The world of Becoming does not have full existence. For
Plato it is always about to exist, this is the very nature of Becoming. As
I have argued earlier, the soul is also not a mere product of the cosmos.
Soul does not arise out of the cosmic order alone. It is not the mere
product of Necessity, though Necessity constrained its development.
The soul is not of the cosmos, but it is an integral part of the cosmos. It
can never exist anywhere else. Human soul will never exist as human
soul in the World of Being. It has never been there and it could never
be there. It is necessarily part of the world of Becoming.

Plato has created one great cosmic animal, the world of
Becoming. Each distinct part of this cosmic animal shares certain
features. In that sense, the cosmos is whole and one. Even in its
becoming state, the visible world is fundamentally one. In what sense
and to what degree is this unity seen? For Plato, the objects of the
world of Becoming are those things that fail to be "absolute, constant,
and unchanging" in the strongest sense of those terms.[180] I have already
argued that, as a created thing, soul cannot have all these attributes in
the strongest possible sense. Let me try to formalize what I believe
Plato to be saying about the cosmic unity of the soul and the physical
make-up of the universe:

If x is part of the cosmos, then it is necessary that the
following propositions be true of x at all times:

1. "X is coming into being as opposed to the states described by 'to be' or 'not to be.'"
   1.1. "It is necessary that x will never fully be."
   1.2. "It is possible for any x, that x can cease to come into being and therefore come to 'not be.'"
   1.3. "It is possible for any object x in the cosmos that x will never in fact cease to come into being."
   1.4. "There are two possible ways for x to come into being, it can be a thing changing in terms of location or being:"
      1.4.1. "Either x is always moving, and causing motion, and hence never coming to be..."
      1.4.2. "Or x is always changing its fundamental attributes (color, size, hardness and the like) and hence never coming to be."
2. "For any object x, x is not a Form."
3. "For any object x, x is not strongly and necessarily simple."
   3.1. "It is possible that any object x, be AS simple."
      3.1.1. "Immortal soul is AS simple"
      3.1.2. "Matter is complex by nature and not simple."[181]
4. "For any object x, x will appear to have an age."
   4.1. "It is possible for any object x, that x will actually have the age it appears to have."
   4.2. "It is possible for any object x, that x will not have the age it appears to have."

The cosmos is, therefore, composed of only one sort of thing: that thing which possesses attributes one through four. There is room for difference between matter and soul in that unity, because of the difference in how the two undergo the process of becoming. I have argued that soul corresponds to 1.4.1. Later I will try to prove that matter is captured by the description at 1.4.2. Soul is most like the Forms of anything in the world of Becoming, because it has AS simplicity and remains constant as to its essence. Matter is least like the Forms because it is complex and undergoes fundamental change in its nature over time. Plato has, therefore, presented a cosmic order that is at once unified in becoming, but has two distinct parts in terms of the means by which it experiences becoming.

The importance of this to the human is plain. The soul and the body are not different in terms of their substance. They are both essentially becoming things. They are different in the process of becoming. Soul is motion in a circle. What is the body? I have described it as that which is undergoing change in its fundamental attributes. In briefly examining this idea as it appears in the *Timaeus*, Plato will be revealed as a dualist in a weak sense.

Motion, Soul, and Matter

Our earlier discussions, while precise about the nature of the soul, were imprecise about the nature of the body. Given the importance of the relationship of the soul to the body, I will try briefly to describe the status of the body in *Timaeus*. Of course, the human body is made of matter and so an understanding of the nature of the body, must begin with an understanding of the Platonic idea of matter.

Like everything else in the world of Becoming, body or matter never is. It is always undergoing motion from forces or laws external to it. This motion causes any given bit of it to undergo almost constant change as to its basic attributes. First, it may be water and cool. Then it may become fire and become hot. Plato is clearly concerned about the Parmenidean paradox.

Parmenides had said,

> The one, that it is and that it is impossible for it not to be is the path of Persuasion; the other, that it is not and that is needful that it not be, that I declare to you in an altogether indiscernible track: for you could not know what is not – that cannot be done – nor indicate it.[182]

He had also said, "What is there to be said and thought must needs be: for it is there for being but nothing is not."[183] He was deeply interested in the distinction between is and is not. Parmenides had finally claimed as a result of his thinking, "... coming to be is extinguished and perishing unheard of."[184] Of course, the paradox is that the visible world seems full of just those very things. The things of the material world appear to be constantly coming and perishing. Parmenides had made this paradox even more difficult, as we have seen, by denying that one could even talk sensibly about things that are not.

      This paradox or problem was clearly on Plato's mind from the start of the *Timaeus*. At 28, the distinction between Becoming and Being is made. It is a distinction to be made "first of all."[185] In Becoming, Plato believed he had found a way around the Parmenidean paradox. Becoming things are not, strictly speaking, nor are they strictly not. They are between, going one way and then another.[186] It is, perhaps, possible to talk about them for this very reason, though it is not possible to have sure knowledge of such transient "things."[187]

      Plato wants to deny full "Being" to the body, which goes through change. On the other hand, he must explain the appearances of the world around him. Things have a "seeming" existence. His theory of matter, which is intrinsically tied to his psychology, will try to answer Parmenides while making sense out of the appearances of the natural world. A sketch of Plato's view in outline form will provide a better understanding of the relationship between soul and body.

      Strictly speaking, for Plato, the motion of any given body is a combination of the first movement of soul combined with the natural tendency of like to move to like.[188] Matter cannot first move without soul, but once motion is established the physical law[189] of like to like can guide or force certain motions. Motion can, therefore, be proper or improper. Proper motion is in accord with the reasonable motion of soul. Improper motion results from the unreasoning attraction of like to like. This improper motion contends with reason.

      Soul and body are, therefore, in tension at times. Matter, which needs soul to move, does not always submit to the order of motion proper to soul. On the other hand, both soul and body are dependent on each other. Soul needs body to incarnate its motion in a reasoning animal (either human or cosmic).[190] Plato has pictured the cosmos in constant creative tension. His cosmology is the result of taking seriously the notion that the overarching principle of the *Timaeus* is the fact that the cosmos is a becoming, not an is.

      All of this is helpful in understanding the relationship of the soul, motion, and the body in *Timaeus*. I have argued earlier that soul can be confused or deterred in its primary motion. One way this could happen is for the natural tendencies of matter to overcome the motions of the soul. Plato has given the first cause of motion as the the self-moving soul. But that is not the whole picture, "the facts about (motion and rest) have already been stated in part, but in addition thereto we must state further that motion never consents to exist within uniformity."[191] He explains, "Accordingly, we must always place rest in uniformity. The cause of the non-uniform nature lies in inequality."[192] In a universe where things are mixed, as is especially true in the sub-lunar realm, matter constantly desires homogeneity. On the other hand, in the jumble of the elements, final uniformity would be impossible. As Plato points out at 58b, pockets of substance would be transformed from one primary element (air, fire, water)[193] to another.

This transformation would change the direction of matter's impulse of "like to like." Water drawn to the main mass of water might run into some fire that would break it up. This would produce particles of air or fire, and "like to like" would change the direction of the particles in relation to the universe. What once was being drawn to water is now being drawn to fire or air, depending on the new formulation of the matter. This attraction is not reasonable, it is the process of necessity. This has a direct implication for the relationship between the body and the soul in a human being. If this view of matter is correct, then dominating matter with a proper motion will be nearly impossible for soul. There will often be a contrary motion produced by the very nature of matter.

What happens to a human when the reasonable direction to a proper motion in their souls is overcome by these attractions? In simple pictorial language, they have sick souls, overcome by inappropriate change: "weakening,"[194] "vapors,"[195] or "massiveness."[196]

The bodies of the world of Becoming are nothing like the Forms. It is necessary that the Forms do not move. It is not possible that they move. They have no potential for motion. They already are, do not move, therefore they will never move. On the other hand, the bodies of the cosmos do have such a motion. In this way, they are like the soul and unlike the Forms. Bodies and soul are alike in this case: both move constantly.

Bodies are even less like the Forms, however. The soul has one fundamental circular motion to which it wishes to return. The body has no such basic nature. It undergoes change all the time about the direction in which it desires to move. It has no lasting attributes. In this way, one can see again that the soul is most like the Forms. There is much more that could be said about the nature of matter in *Timaeus*, but this brief introduction is sufficient to make one vital point about the nature of the human in the dialogue.

The human body, made of this shifting matter, has nothing in common with the Forms. Soul in the sub-lunar realm will never fully tame the contrary impulses of matter within the human body. Soul and matter will often be in some tension, with soul desiring pure circular motion and matter striving to move to like matter. There is, therefore, good reason to think that Plato is a dualist in his view of these characteristics.[197]

Humanity and Dualism

In his examination of dualism Plato has raised two important points. In what way? If by dualism, it is meant that the human body is composed of two major functioning parts (soul and body), then Plato is indeed a dualist. Neither the soul nor the body can be reduced to the other. Plato is neither a materialist nor an idealist regarding humankind. Humans are fundamentally neither bodies nor souls. To be human is to be a soul incarnate in something, having a body, even if that body is a star.

On the other hand, I opened this discussion of dualism with Plato's views about reality that place an important limitation on his dualism. If the dualist's claim is the stronger one, that the human consists of two parts that are dissimilar, then it has already been shown in what way Plato's cosmos is not dualistic. Human soul, soul-system, and body are in the same state: coming into being. They are merely different ways of manifesting the process of coming into Being. Since there is no real substance in the world of Becoming, saying that they are the same substance is not accurate. Plato cannot, therefore, be a monist about the cosmos. Rather, one must say that they are different ways of becoming substance. Plato would be a dualist if matter or soul could ever actually exist, but neither thing ever achieves such a state. Both are evolving in the nether world between full Being and not Being.

This brings Plato to the classic problem of the interaction between soul and body in systems that are dualistic. Thilly describes the problem, "It is also inexplicable how ... a pure spirit, should be able to impart motion to matter." He says of soul and matter, "If (they) are two distinct categories, there can be no real converse between them."[198] This problem that haunts strongly dualistic systems like that of Descartes is not as great a problem for Plato's dualism.

Soul, take as a soul-system,[199] and body can, for Plato, sensibly interact if anything can interact within the Platonic cosmos. Soul and body are the same sort of thing. Both are becoming things. As I have argued earlier, soul is a self-moving thing with the potential to move other things. It never rests, so it never reaches a place where one can say it is. Body, strictly speaking, is the thing moved in such and such a direction by soul. In this motion, it undergoes change at the atomic level of its being.[200] It is in a constant state of reformulation, driven to this by the reason of the soul and by the necessity of its own nature and of space. Both body and soul, even in a human, reduce to one ontological category: becoming.

Can becoming things interact? Some systems solve the problem of interaction by reducing one thing to another, soul to body or body to soul. Plato does not take this out. There are, for Plato, two types of becoming things: soul and body. These categories within the class becoming are not reducible to each other. Soul will never be "becoming body." Body will never be "becoming soul." On the other hand, given their ontological unity, it is not clear why soul and body should not be able to interact. As Thilly points out, the problem for Descartes was caused by the fundamental distinction in his system between soul, God, and matter.[201] There was no possible   point of contact for soul and matter.

For Plato, this is simply not so. As I have shown, soul and body have many things in common: both can move,[202] both are subject to change,[203] and both are dependent on the Forms for existence .[204] Soul is that which moves body or matter. Body or matter is the thing moved. Intellectual activity takes place during that interaction. This is always true, as the soul is either in the body of a star or in the body of an animal.[205] Intellectual activity in   *Timaeus* is tied to the motion of the soul.[206]

It is, of course, difficult to understand how intellectual activity could be reduced to motion in a body. This is, however, what Plato believed.[207] Can sense be made of this reduction? If so, then Plato has successfully provided for soul and body in a way that skirts the Cartesian problem. It is beyond the scope of the current examination of the nature of the soul to explore this question about what the soul does.

Plato has not solved the problem of Cartesian dualism, but then Plato is not a Cartesian dualist. Plato does have a form of dualism for humans, but not one subject to the classic formulation of the objection. If Plato's distinction between "is," "becoming," and "is not" is sound, then the psychology of the *Timaeus* is a form of psychological dualism not subject to Cartesian problems.

Death and Memory

A more serious problem for understanding Plato's psychology

is the problem of memory. It is basic to Platonic doctrine that humans remember their life on the astral plane.[208] Given the psychology of the *Timaeus*, how could the soul accumulate memories? It is important to notice that this is a problem for a soul on even a Cartesian reading of Plato. A disembodied person has no more obvious capability to remember than the self-moving being that I have described. Plato has a problem with memory, but it is not a problem that is unique to my reading of the Platonic psychology.

One tentative suggestion, based on the notion of recollection, is that a relationship with an eternal Form "marks" the subject and changes its own abilities in important ways. This follows the image that Socrates uses in *Theatetus* 191c and following. First, he compares memory to a wax block on which impressions can be made. He says:

> The only possibility of erroneous opinion is, when knowing you and Theodorus, and having on the waxen block the impression of both of you given as by a seal, but seeing you imperfectly and at a distance, I try to assign the right impression of memory to the right visual impression, and to fit this into its own print: if I succeed, recognition will take place; but if I fail and transpose them, putting the foot into the wrong shoe--that is to say, putting the vision of either of you on to the wrong impression, or if my mind, like the sight in a mirror, which is transferred from right to left, err by reason of some similar affection, then "heterodoxy" and false opinion ensues.

This picture of the wax as memory, a brilliant teaching tool in the context of a dialogue on epistemology, can be translated without too much difficulty into the cosmological terms of the *Timaeus*.[209] Once a soul has been in a relationship with Beauty, it is something that was, at one time, becoming-beautiful. It may be easier for a soul in this position to enter into such a relationship again. Its capacity to recognize certain directions and to be the catalyst to certain sorts of beautiful motions may be increased. Experience of this sort may lead to an increased ability or receptivity to experiencing that thing again. One can only resort to the language of the *Timaeus* in describing what this might mean. It might be that the relationship with a Form strengthens certain motions of the soul[210] and thus increases its ability to resist non-circular motions.

Of course, one can leave a lasting impression on a thing that is becoming. A child can be shaped even as he exits the womb, before he is in the strong sense. Can this picture of memory be translated into more mathematical or physical terms? I think that it can. The *Cratylus* gives the reader a clue when Socrates says, "memory, as any one may see, expresses rest in the soul, and not motion."[211] This is an interesting notion that may help make sense of the association between soul and memory. If a soul is in a relationship with a physical object or a Form at time t, then it is always going to be the case that the soul was in that relationship at t. No matter what happens to the soul at time t+1, the past cannot be changed. The memory of that time, the experience, is a permanent part of the evolving history of that soul.

The past of the soul is more at rest than standard relationships in becoming, in the sense that past relationships cannot change. The past of becoming does not become full Being, however, because the past itself is never complete. More past is always becoming part of the set of things that have happened in the world of Becoming. The past is never complete. A memory itself, therefore, undergoes limited change in its changing relationship to the past itself. As more relationships become past relationships, the status of an event in memory changes. Minimally, the past event, which was "n" number of relationships ago, is now "n+1" ago. Memory, like soul, is therefore somewhat like the Forms, but not an unchanging Form.

How can a becoming soul be marked?[212] After all, the notion of becoming is a notion of change. How could a soul retain these marks during the process of change? What are these marks? To solve this problem, I would urge the reader to view the marks as a strengthening of proper motion in the soul. As I have shown earlier, Plato clearly believes there are actions humans can take to "bring right" or strengthen the divine soul's motions. Such benefits would be lasting, at least until negated by contrary motions. When confronted with a new bit of matter or motion, this strengthening of right motion would enable the soul to make a better judgment about that new matter or motion. This could be conceived of as a result of the earlier positive relationship. In the same way, a negative memory or a weakened soul brought on by detrimental relationships with matter could cause the soul to make bad judgments.

These memories would not have everlasting effects. A soul could not retain memories forever. Enough contact with contrary motions or matter that is not pliable would destroy a soul's ability to benefit from a previous positive relationship. In other words, enough negative motion could counter all the positive gains from a past experience and negate the value of that relationship. Humans would "forget" or lose the benefit of the past experience. On the other hand, one positive experience would tend to draw the person toward the objects or motions that helped.

On the idea that "like is drawn to like," a soul fed on good food and study will have a brain full of material that will be drawn to more things of like nature. This is the start of a very crude cosmological and psychological picture of learning. In any case, I have attempted to sketch the first rough outlines of what a Platonic theory of memory would look like based on the data in the text. Plato says nothing about the issue directly, so it cannot be finally resolved.

An object in the world of Becoming would not have to be self-aware to utilize such problem-solving methods. Contemporary scientists use such language to describe the learning that takes place in certain non-rational objects. Richard Dawkins, in his book *The Blind Watchmaker*,[213] points out that in biologic   al research many scientists believe that clay forms the basis for the origin of life. Clay that bonds in certain ways produces more clay like itself. In simple terms, the clay that by accident or nature has the ability to reproduce itself in particular circumstances will flourish. This tendency in clay in general will, therefore, be reinforced.

Clay, in a sense, "learns" what it needs to do to survive and reproduce itself. "Appropriate" or "successful" behavior on the part of the clay is rewarded. Soul may go through the same process. Plato says,

> Whoso, then indulges in lusts or in contentions and devotes himself overmuch thereto must of necessity be filled with opinions that are wholly mortal, and altogether, so far as it is possible to become mortal fall not short of this in even a small degree, inasmuch as he has made great his mortal part.[214]

It is important to note that Plato stresses in this passage the filling of the soul-system with opinions. Commentators, enamored by cosmological detail, frequently fail to note that even in this section Plato is most concerned about relationships within the soul to the Forms. His is not a cosmology just of the physical, because he does not believe the physical exists in the strong sense. The soul that does badly in the process of reincarnation is the soul locked into what is, perhaps, a self-perpetuating set of improper relationships with the things that cannot be true.

On the positive side, coming into relationship with certain Forms may change the soul's disposition and put it in a better position for future encounters of the same sort. There is no evidence that the Platonic soul is self-aware. How could memory retain literal physical "marks" like wax? It does seem it could keep increased or decreased ability to perform its primary function. Memory is simply the created disposition from a past encounter to recognize and desire more encounters like the first.

Once again, it should be stated that Plato does not deal directly with this or many other psychological questions. He does believe humans remember. He does not describe in detail how that process is supposed to work. I have tried to suggest one way out for him, based on clues in the dialogues.

Conclusion: Plato's View of the Human Soul

What is the reader to make of the account of the soul in the *Timaeus*? First, the immortal portion of the human soul is AS simple. As we have seen, this gives the soul the potential for true, though accidental, immortality. This conclusion is supported by the rest of the Platonic corpus, especially the *Phaedo*. The soul taken as the functioning psychic unit in the visible human is not simple. It contains the mortal soul. The mortal part of the soul is capable of death. It may survive for a moment after the death of the body, but does not have immortal life in the *Timaeus*.

Second, the human soul has the appearance of being the first-born. It will always seem to be the primary cause of all human or animal motion, even if there were no actual first humans. The soul and the soul-system have only an apparent priority in time.

Third, the concept of soul acts as the self-moving cause of motion within the Platonic cosmology. It is becoming in the sense of always moving. Matter is also a becoming thing. It consists of a series of changing properties in space. A bit of matter can be moved by soul. Matter and soul cannot be reduced to each other, but they are both becoming things. They express this becoming in different ways.

Therefore this is not a Christian soul, a ghost in the body. Both body and soul for Plato are more abstract than they became in later Christian neo-Platonic thought.[215] For Plato, soul is the fundamental explanation for motion, though he will allow for other impulses to direct this motion once the cosmos is set moving by soul. Both body and soul are part of the world of Becoming. This median position between "is" and "is not" is the fundamental fact of the Platonic psychology.

Without using the *Timaeus* as the starting point for understanding the Platonic soul, it is easy to view the word "soul" as referring only to the immortal soul of the *Phaedo* or only to the soul-system of the *Republic*. The two images can seem contradictory. The *Timaeus* provides an overall psychology that accounts for both images of the soul.

If one does not get lost in the details of the cosmological model, but continues to look for the position of Becoming between non-existence and Being, then a rich and useful psychology manifests itself. Using *Timaeus* as a starting point, the reader sees that intellect itself, for Plato, is for orderly and ordering motion. She finds a place for the work of the intellect in both the life of the cosmos and the city-state. The human, for Plato, is possessed by a divine spirit.[216] This divine spirit, the soul, is the human's link to the real world of the Forms. The soul, however, does its work as part of a soul-system. This system is easy to confuse with the divine soul itself, if care is not taken.

The soul-system is described as immortal and mortal in the dialogue. The mortal and immortal parts are given two separate creation stories. I have suggested that in the *Timaeus*, Plato uses the word "soul" to refer to three things:

1. The divine soul element[217]
2. The mortal soul element[218]
3. The divine soul and the human soul as a functioning unit (the soul-system).[219]

The first account of the human soul in *Timaeus*, from 41d to 42d, details the creation of the divine soul element. The second account, stretching from 69c to 72d, outlines the creation of the mortal soul element and describes its relation to the divine soul element.

The divine and mortal soul elements are distinct. The divine soul[220] was created by the Father/Creator   , while the mortal soul was constructed by the demigods out of soul-stuff. The mortal soul was built on to the divine soul as another distinct part. It is an element added to the original divine soul to form the new soul-system of the created human being. Plato goes out of his way to stress that the demigods wanted the divine and mortal soul elements kept distinct. The neck, which is very thin compared to the rest of the body, is constructed to keep apart the head, the divine soul element, and the breast, the mortal soul element.[221]

Why does this work? The soul is only confused if it comes into contact with matter or motion that it cannot handle. The narrowness of the neck and the thickness of the skull prevent the soul from being utterly overwhelmed by relationships with matter. Once set moving, matter has the potential to swerve mechanistically on its own. It cannot move on its own, but it can provide its own natural direction. This direction can also cause problems for the immortal soul.

The distinctions between the mortal and the immortal can, however, be overemphasized. The divine soul and the mortal soul do work together. They are a functional whole, a soul-system. There is no way for humans to see the immortal soul functioning without the mortal soul except in the astral realm. Plato usually refers to this entire working system as simply the human soul.

What does this soul-system do in the body? If my reading of the *Timaeus* is correct, then the soul-system does what soul must do. It provides motion to the body. This notion is not foreign to other dialogues. According to the *Laws* of Plato, the soul is the "self-generated motion of the body."[222] In functional terms, when the human is embodied and living, it is proper to think of the mortal and divine soul as one soul-system carrying out the one soul task with all its ramifications. These parts are an essential unity, though not a simple unity. Each part of the soul-system, of course, has subsidiary functions that contribute to achieving the overall purpose of the soul in the body. This does not mitigate against the overall functional unity of the soul. Different locations in the functioning soul carry out different sub-tasks, but each of these sub-tasks is part of the one project of creating a living, rational being.

The picture of the human soul in *Timaeus* is a subtle and rich one. Using this view, I will be able to demonstrate in the chapter that follows that Plato has developed a psychology in the *Timaeus* that is consistent with his other writings. Not only is it consistent with other dialogues, but it enriches the reading of those dialogues. This psychology throws light on difficulties that have traditionally been ascribed to Plato's view of the human soul. This complex account of how the human really works is, at worst, a likely story. At its most important points, detailing the actions of the soul in man, it is what Plato believed to be the closest thing to truth available in the world of Becoming. The view of the human soul in the *Timaeus* is truly the key to unlocking the Platonic psychology.

---

[1] Cornford, 11. "... we are evidently not to imagine that Socrates has, on the previous day, narrated the whole conversation of the *Republic* or any part of it."

---

[2] A. E. Taylor and R.G. Bury claim that this section is a summary of the first part of *Republic*. In his comment before the section Desmond Lee sees that it is "very like" the *Republic*. Taylor, 13. Bury, R.G. "Introduction" in *Timaeus*. Translated by R.G. Bury. (Cambridge, Mass.: Harvard University Press), 3. Lee, Desmond. "Notes" in *Timaeus and Critias*. Translated by Desmond Lee. (New York: Penguin Books, 1971), 27.

[3] *Timaeus* 27a.

[4] *Timaeus* 28a.

[5] *Timaeus* 28b.

[6] A bad habit of some translators is to place "god" in their translation where the text does not use it for the work of the craftsman of the universe. A.E. Taylor is often guilty of this. Francis Cornford's translation is quite careful in this regard.

[7] This constraint is only explained later in the dialogue.

[8] *Timaeus* 29c.

[9] In this I imitate the attitude of Francis Cornford, who points out that one can come to theistic and pantheistic conclusions based on the text. It is, therefore, best to refrain from coming to conclusions in this regard at all. Cornford, 39. "We shall do better to hold back from this or any other conclusion (related to the status of the Demiurge) and confine our attention to the world with its body and soul and the reason they contain."

[10] Augustine, for example, fell into this confusion in book 11, chapter 21 of *City of God*.

[11] Cornford, 24-25.

[12] *Timaeus* 30b.

[13] Bremmer, Jan. *The Early Greek Concept of the Soul* (Princeton: Princeton University Press, 1983), 66-67.

[14] ibid.

[15] Kirk, G.S., Raven, J.E., and Schoefield, M. *The Presocratic Philosophers* (Cambridge: Cambridge University Press, 1983) 96-97.

[16] Kirk, 204-205.

[17] Of course, Plato would have to contend with thinkers like Heraclitus who believed the soul to be made of "fiery ether." This physical substance would be only accidentally invisible.

[18] This in fact was how neo-Platonists like Plotinus often viewed the situation.

[19] Kirk, 241.

[20] *Timaeus* 29d.

[21] *Timaeus* 29c.

[22] *Timaeus* 30a.

[23] *Timaeus* 32c. The notion of space or plastic is introduced later.

[24] *Timaeus* 32c (Bury translation).

[25] *Timaeus* 34a. (Bury translation).

[26] ibid.

[27] *Timaeus* 34b.

[28] Cornford, 62.

[29] Bury, 66.

[30] Taylor, 107.

[31] *Timaeus* 35b.

[32] *Timaeus* 35b.

[33] *Phaedo* 83e.

[34] See, for example: Aquinas, Thomas.   *Summa Theologica* in *Introduction to St. Thomas Aquinas*. Edited by Anton C. Pegis (New York: Modern Library, 1948), question III. For a recent discussion see: Mann, William E. "Simplicity and Immutability in God" in *The Concept of God* edited by Thomas V. Morris (Oxford: Oxford University Press, 1987), 253-267.

[35] I place "formed" in quotation marks, because here I run into the issue of whether Plato believed in an actual creation or not. Is this process once-upon-a-time or a continuous event? That is not clear.

[36] *Timaeus* 35b.

[37] *Timaeus* 35.

[38] *Timaeus* 35b (Bury).

[39] Aristotle, *On Generation and Corruption* 315b.

[40] See in particular Aristotle   's discussion related to combination in   *On Generation and Corruption* at 328.

[41] *Timaeus* 36d.

[42] *Timaeus* 37 and numerous other places.

[43] I am not referring to a line segment, but to a line extending infinitely in both directions.

[44] *Timaeus* 37d, where Plato says that immortality cannot be attached in "its entirety to that which is generated" (Bury), is but one example.

[45] *Timaeus* 42b.

[46] See for example *Phaedo* 80b.

[47] *Cratylus* 400a (Jowett).

[48] *Laws* 895e10 (Pangle).

[49] *Timaeus* 34a.

[50] *Timaeus* 38e. I will have more to say about the creation of the soul and time later.

[51] Robinson, T.M. Unpublished paper given at Cornell University, November 1994.

[52] In talking about human soul, I also include the soul of all animals. I will have more to say about this at a later point.

[53] *Timaeus* 40b.

[54] Of course, for the soul these motions are less natural.

[55] *De Anima* 407a.

[56] I would understand this "giving" in the context of the entire creation account. The Demiurge would "appoint" a motion by bringing soul into contact with certain sorts of matter.

[57] See *Timaeus* 43b where the rational soul, fresh from its star, comes into contact with the many motions of the lower sphere. Recall that almost all the motions in the lower sphere are also caused by soul, but a soul that is not performing, or capable of performing, the work of reason. There is some

suggestion at 53 that there is a "natural" motion apart from soul in the attraction of like particles to like. Further discussion on this interesting point is beyond the scope of this work. Taylor provides one interesting reading in his *Commentary*, 355-356.

[58] *Timaeus* 53c.

[59] I will have more to say about this relationship later. Matter will eventually be understood differently than the simple manner in which it is presented at this point.

[60] I will have more to say about this later.

[61] Philosophers of science will be familiar with an informal version of this concept from the work of Philip Gosse, the late Victorian scientist and theologian. He introduced the idea in his work *Omphalos*. This is noted by Stephen G. Brush in his article "Ghosts from the Nineteenth Century," in *Scientists Confront Creationism* (New York: W.W. Norton, 1983), 55.

[62] This is not to commit to the notion that it exists as a discrete unit of time. In a universe that is coming into being, any moment is the moment of creation.

[63] Cornford, 101.

[64] Cornford, 105.

[65] *Timaeus* 39e-40e.

[66] I will use this term to parallel the biological notion of "ecosystem." An individual psycho system is a unique and contained set of physical constraints in which a particular soul is contained.

[67] The examples in *Critias* (109b-110a) and *Timaeus* itself are good clues in this regard. Both assume a past for humankind stretching into the far reaches of eternity. The Egyptian priest scoffs at the notion of Phoroneus as first man at *Timaeus* 22b.

[68] *Timaeus* 41b (Lee).

[69] Taylor, 255.

[70] The gods are engaged in molding, framing, and controlling the other parts of the human soul. They do not "create" these parts. The material has been provided to them in an unfinished state, but it has been provided.

[71] It is no accident that *Timaeus* 41e speaks of a purity that is "but the second and third degree." The mortal/immortal soul construct will have three parts.

[72] *Timaeus* 48e and following.

[73] See *Republic* X and the Myth of Er for an example not drawn from the *Timaeus*.

[74] *Timaeus* 41e.

[75] *Timaeus* 41e-42b.

[76] *Timaeus* 42d.

[77] *Timaeus* 42.

[78] *Timaeus* 41e (Bury).

[79] *Timaeus* 42a (Bury).

[80] This is a disturbing claim from the author of the more egalitarian *Republic*.

[81] *Timaeus* 69d.

[82] See especially *Republic* 451c-453d.

---

[83] *Timaeus* 69c.

[84] *Timaeus* 44.

[85] *Timaeus* 44.

[86] *Timaeus* 44c.

[87] *Timaeus* 86-87.

[88] *Timaeus* 49.

[89] In a private conversation, Thomas Robinson   , a well-known Platonic commentator, said that a modern could best think of this term as referring to the plastic of the universe.

[90] Immortality and simplicity are in a bi-conditional relationship for Plato.

[91] I will have more to say about this later.

[92] Let me be clear on a point: soul is needed to rationally move an object. Once that object is moving Necessity (laws that govern particles) tend to want to direct that motion.

[93] *Timaeus* 47b.

[94] *Republic* 527d.

[95] *Timaeus* 63e. See also Plato's picture of respiration and vision at 67 for examples of the use of this doctrine in Plato that even Taylor accepts as genuine.

[96] Cornford, 239-246. Taylor disagrees with Cornford . He does not admit any non-psychological motion in the universe (*Commentary* 440-445). He seems to have as a motive hostility to Aristotle as a scientist: "... it is a tragedy of the human intellect that Aristotle and the Stoics, with their crude Ionian prepossessions, were able to arrest the tendency (toward scientific understanding) as thoroughly as they did." He cannot bear any form of this "Ionian" reasoning in Plato. This is not, however, an argument and the text itself does not lend Taylor much support. So though I agree with Taylor about the soul and motion, I am not happy with his argument.

[97] *Timaeus* 43c.

[98] *Timaeus* 42b and 43b. "... since it partook of all the six motions...."

[99] Inability to move earth, water, and air easily is suggested at 43c as quoted. In the story of reincarnation the notion that a "fleshy" soul has great difficulty suggests that "amount" of substance also matters. *Timaeus* 90b-c.

[100] To avoid being overly cumbersome, I will say that "like to like" and the pressure of the cosmic sphere inward are "motions." Strictly speaking, they are impulses to move irrationally that occur in matter with a soul. The soul is moving the object, not the impulse to move in x direction.

[101] This is argued for earlier. My conclusions are based primarily on the behavior of the stars and cosmic soul at *Timaeus* 39, the notion of simplicity of the soul (implied by its immortality and the Platonic idea that composites cannot be immortal seen at *Phaedo* 78c), the fact that only circular motions are divine (*Timaeus* 44d), other Platonic definitions of soul (*Laws* 895e10), and the goal of circular motion within the human head (*Timaeus* 44d).

[102] This is the consistent Platonic doctrine (clearly seen at   *Laws* 895e10) that the soul is self-moved and imparts motion to other things.

---

[103] With Cornford , I take this to be the implication of 52d-53c. Reason acts to check these chaotic impulses, but they exist in the world of Becoming.

[104] I would argue that this implied by the confusion of the motions of the head by the five contrary "motions" of the world of Becoming at *Timaeus* 43c.

[105] I believe that this is implied by *Timaeus* 90b-e. It is possible to not "indulge in lusts" and so bring the motions of the head back into proper order. It is possible, according to this passage, to master the contrary motions and not to be mastered by them. I will have more to say about this later, but Plato clearly makes "righting" the soul a physical problem with a physical solution at 86 and 87.

[106] *Timaeus* 43c. Note the reference to earth, which is given no motion. Earth itself seems too difficult to move properly apart from any confused motions it may come with.

[107] It is simply the nature of soul to move ... if it cannot move in a circle, then it will still move. See *Timaeus* 43e where the rational soul moves "irrationally."

[108] All stars move with the motion of the same (*Timaeus* 36c) and all planets with the motion of the other (*Timaeus* 36d). Both motions are circular.

[109] This is the implication of the restoration of proper motion mentioned at 90d.

[110] Circular motion is not attributed to any other part of the body in the text.

[111] *Timaeus* 60.

[112] One, of course, should not anticipate "perfection" in the world of Becoming . Necessity is a recalcitrant foe.

[113] In a paper I heard at Cornell University, T.M. Robinson claimed that Plato's cosmology may be quite close to several concepts found in modern physics. It would not be surprising if his program were equally illuminating to issues of biological origins. In any case, Plato is quick to remind the reader that the examination of such issues is a "recreation" and a "pleasure not to be repented of." He prompts the reader yet again to recall that his description is "a likely story." *Timaeus* 48d.

[114] *Symposium* 207d.

[115] *Timaeus* 65b.

[116] *Timaeus* 69c.

[117] *Timaeus* 69. It is important to note that they do not create the mortal soul substance itself. They "build" a mortal soul. This is in line with my suggestion earlier that the God has provided them with the raw materials and the place to make such a soul. Again, religious language can obscure the fact that both the mortal and the immortal soul are co-eternal. They come "into being" together.

[118] *Timaeus* 69d.

[119] *Timaeus* 69-70.

[120] *Timaeus* 70.

[121] *Timaeus* 70-71.

[122] *Republic* 496-497.

[123] ibid.

[124] *Timaeus* 69e.

[125] Taylor, 512.

[126] Cornford, 289.

[127] Taylor, 513.

[128] For an interesting collection of oracles see Robin Fox' outstanding book *Pagans and Christians* (New York: Alfred A. Knopf, 1986).

[129] Ibid.

[130] Morford, Mark P.O. and Lenardon , Robert. *Classical Mythology* (New York: Longman, 1991), 193.

[131] *Timaeus* 71e.

[132] Burkert , Walter. *Greek Religion* (Cambridge: Harvard University Press, 1985) 116.

[133] ibid.

[134] See the rationalistic hermeneutic proposed in Peter Van Inwagen's "Genesis and Evolution" in *Reasoned Faith*. Edited by Eleonore Stump, (Cornell: Cornell University Press, 1993), 91-127.

[135] *Timaeus* 72b.

[136] *Timaeus* 71b.

[137] Why would this mistranslation have happened? People have been aware of the contents of the oracle, in the form of a riddle, since ancient times. Why then were the roles of the women at Delphi demeaned?

[138] *Timaeus* 72d (Bury).

[139] What Plato believed should be loved in Socrates   is made clear in *Symposium*.

[140] *Timaeus* 87.

[141] An example other than those within the *Timaeus* can be found in the Myth of Er at the end of the *Republic* 612b- 621d.

[142] See again the *Symposium* 211.

[143] *Timaeus* 73e.

[144] Plato notes that one exception might be the intelligence or soul found in the boneless tongue. This may be a case of flesh binding marrow.

[145] *Timaeus* 73d.

[146] See especially the appeal of Glaucon at the start of Book II in *Republic*.

[147] *Timaeus* 20.

[148] *Timaeus* 73b.

[149] See for example *Timaeus* 91e and the discussion of the heads of those who will become four-footed beasts.

[150] Since free from matter, it would return to its natural and proper motion.

[151] *Timaeus* 90b (Bury).

[152] *Timaeus* 90d.

[153] *Timaeus* 87c-89d.

[154] See especially 616 to the end.

[155] Popper, Karl. *Popper Selections*. Edited by David Miller (Princeton: Princeton University Press, 1985.), 74. In the context, Popper is discussing Plato's epistemology, but he develops the charge in a manner that would apply to his cosmology.

[156] By "living creature," I mean just those creatures that have souls.

[157] I am in debt to Professor Modrak for her comments on this point.

[158] *Timaeus* 72d (Bury).

[159] *Republic* 375 band following.

[160] The plausibility of the entire reincarnation story at   *Timaeus* 92 depends on this knowledge on our part.

[161] Some of the neo-Platonists accepted the implications of these views.

[162] *Laws* 798a (Pangle).

[163] *Timaeus* 86e.

[164] *Laws* 782e.

[165] This is derived for the most part from the *Laws*.

[166] This is derived from the earlier arguments regarding the soul in *Timaeus*.

[167] *Phaedo* 62.

[168] *Laws* 732c (Pangle).

[169] Pangle, 475.

[170] Pangle is a Straussian in not wanting to attribute the views of the Athenian stranger to Plato. I have, of course, rejected that course. It is fair to say, in any case, that Pangle reads the text as synthesis of two extremes, while I read it as a comparison of one "bad" to another.

[171] Pangle, like many other Straussians, fails to respect other commentators because their "literature approaches Plato in the light of modern preconceptions (Pangle, xiii)." At the same time, it is arguable that they merely import older preconceptions into the text. This might explain Pangle's failure to correctly read this text.

[172] *Timaeus* 77c.

[173] *Timaeus* 77b-c.

[174] Hippocrates, *On Ancient Medicine* translated by Francis Adams in the Library of the Future (R) Series Third Edition Windows (TM) Version 4.2.

[175] Deborah Modrak describes Platonists as psychological dualists. Frank Thilly attributes both psychological and substance dualism to Plato. As I shall make clear, I believe Plato was, in fact, a psychological dualist, but that he did not believe in two substances. Modrak, Deborah. *Aristotle: The Power of Perception*. (Chicago: University of Chicago Press, 1987), 44. Thilly, Frank. *A History of Philosophy* (New York: Holt, Rinehart, and Winston, 1961), 81-83.

[176] Thilly, 83.

[177] *Timaeus* 28a-29b and *Phaedo* 65d-66b.

[178] The form of the Good suggests itself.

[179] Once again I am not committed to the coherence of this picture. I am simply arguing that it is the picture that Plato presents in the *Timaeus*.

[180] *Phaedo* 79d.

[181] I will have more to say about this later in a brief discussion of the nature of matter. The complexity of matter is clearly implied in the account of matter at *Timaeus* 53c-57d.

[182] *Parmenides* 291.

[183] *Parmenides* 293.

[184] *Parmenides* 296.

---

[185] *Timaeus* 28.

[186] *Timaeus* 29.

[187] *Timaeus* 28-30.

[188] Once the cosmic animal, or human animal, is moving, then the natural law of "like drawn to like" comes into play. A piece of fire is drawn towards a larger amount of fire. This is the problem of necessity. Reason gets things going, but cannot always control where they go on all levels. See *Timaeus* 57d.

[189] A given natural law is a particular disposition to impact the motion of the soul in a particular way.

[190] *Timaeus* 30b. The "best" thing for the cosmos is to be formed into a cosmic animal: a soul in a body. How could this fail to be best for humans? Once again Plato's thought moves from the macro- to the micro-level.

[191] *Timaeus* 58a.

[192] *Timaeus* 58a-b.

[193] Earth cannot be transformed to other elements. It has the odd shape of a cube, not formed from the primary triangles. It can only be broken up to reform into earth at a later time. See *Timaeus* 55e.

[194] *Timaeus* 81d. The basic fire pyramids themselves, after conflict with other particles, can begin to dissolve. It is unclear what they become (line?) or if they can ever be reformulated into "new" sharp pyramids.

[195] *Timaeus* 84e.

[196] *Timaeus* 85d.

[197] By "human" it is important to understand "animal," given Plato's extension of soul to the "lower" species at 91e.

[198] Thilly, 314.

[199] The soul-system consists of the tripartite human soul or, put another way, of the mortal and immortal soul combined.

[200] For a brief description of reformulation of matter see: *Timaeus* 57a-d. Note that in this section matter is driven "like to like" by necessity. We have already noted the motive power of the cosmic soul.

[201] Thilly, 314-316.

[202] Of course, soul moves necessarily itself and body moves only in conjunction with soul. *This difference does not undercut the similarity that both move.*

[203] Soul cannot change in its fundamental nature (circular motion   ), but can undergo change in its relationships with bodies. A soul can move from Socrates to a star.

[204] *Timaeus* 25-27.

[205] *Timaeus* 42 and *Timaeus* 91a-92c.

[206] *Timaeus* 37a and *Timaeus* 41e-42e.

[207] *Timaeus* 37.

[208] In addition to *Timaeus* 41e and following, much of *Meno* is devoted to this topic.

[209] It is important to stress that Plato never does say what knowledge is in the *Theaetetus*.

[210] *Timaeus* 90c and 90d, where he speaks of "tending" the divine part (the

immortal soul).

[211] *Cratylus* 437b.

[212] The *Theatetus* has a seminal discussion of this problem and other related concerns.

[213] Dawkins , Richard. *The Blind Watchmaker* (New York: W.W. Norton, 1987).

[214] *Timaeus* 90c (Bury).

[215] See for example Augustine's notion of the soul and the body in *City of God*. He has conflated Plato with neo-Platonism and misread both at that.

[216] *Timaeus* 90c.

[217] For instance "soul" is used for the divine soul at 42, "... to devise the necessary additions to the soul...."

[218] The mortal soul is called the "soul" at *Timaeus* 70, "the part of the soul which is the seat of courage...."

[219] This is found in the *Timaeus* 72: "this concludes our account of the mortal and divine soul...."

[220] From this point on I will shorten "divine (or mortal) soul element" to divine soul.

[221] *Timaeus* 69-70.

[222] *Laws* 69e.

CHAPTER 3: THE SOUL IMMORTAL AND POLITICAL: THE PSYCHOLOGY OF *TIMAEUS* APPLIED TO THE *PHAEDO* AND THE *REPUBLIC*

In his article, "A Note on Tripartition and Immortality in Plato," Lloyd Gerson comments, "There is a well-known apparent inconsistency in Plato's doctrine of the immortal soul."[1] What is this inconsistency? In the *Phaedo,* the soul is described in terms that are not applicable to the whole soul described in the *Timaeus*. The soul of the *Phaedo* is described as unitary and deathless.[2] Gerson notes, "The *Phaedo* . . . does not teach that the soul is tripartite ...."[3] If one just read the *Phaedo*, it would be easy to reach the conclusion that the whole soul is immortal and that there are no mortal parts.[4]

I wish to apply the results of my investigations into the Platonic notion of soul in *Timaeus* to other Platonic dialogues. Is it consistent with what one finds there? Does it illuminate these texts in new and important ways? Does it perhaps give a means for solving long-standing problems in understanding the arguments of these dialogues? It would be impossible to give a complete answer to these three questions in one work. However, even a brief review of two pivotal dialogues will be sufficient to show that the answer to these questions is almost certainly in the affirmative. In my opinion, two of the most important dialogues to examine in this regard are the *Phaedo* and the *Republic*.[5] Both of these dialogues deal extensively with the issue of human psychology. Each one will present new challenges and support for the psychology I have presented.

Immortality: the Psychology of the *Phaedo*

Phaedo and the Issue of Consistency

According to G.M.A. Grube, the *Phaedo* stands between the early dialogues of Plato and the middle dialogues.[6] This dialogue introduces many notions about the human soul that are important in later dialogues. In some ways, it is seminal to the Platonic psychology. Not only are some of the earliest formulations of Plato's own thinking about the soul found here, but it touches on the notion of immortality in more sustained way than any of the other dialogues. Understanding the context is, however, critical to a full understanding of the dialogue. Plato is not trying simply to show that the some part of Socrates will survive. First, I will attempt to demonstrate that the psychology of the *Phaedo* is consistent with that of the later *Timaeus*. Second, I will examine the dialogue in the light of this psychology to see what fresh insights can be brought out of the text.

In the *Phaedo*, the topic of the soul is introduced in relation to the impending death of Socrates. It will be important to bear this historic context in mind in our discussion.[7] Socrates is attempting to demonstrate to his distraught friends that "I am likely to be right to leave you and my masters here without resentment or complaint, believing that there, as here, I will find good masters and good friends."[8] Cebes, a friend of Socrates, agrees that, based on Socrates' view of the soul, such a willingness to die is excellent. He urges Socrates to argue for his vision of the human soul. The context of the definition of the soul that Plato, through Socrates, presents is an argument in favor of the peaceful death of the philosopher.

What is the description of the soul that Socrates settles on? In *Phaedo* 80b, he describes the soul as, "... most like the divine, deathless, intelligible, uniform, and indissoluble, always the same as itself..." (θείω καὶ ἀθανάτω καὶ νοητῷ καὶ μονοειδεῖ καὶ ἀδιαλύτω καὶ ἀεὶ ὡσαύτως).[9] Socrates holds this position because he believes that each of the characteristics mentioned is necessary to the argument for the immortality of the soul. Understanding this is vital to grasping the force of the argument.

It would appear that the soul described in the *Phaedo* bears little resemblance to the soul Plato depicts in the *Timaeus*. This impression is only superficial, however. There is no real contradiction between the *Phaedo* and the *Timaeus*. The reader must place the descriptive phrases of the *Phaedo* within the theological/cosmological picture of the *Timaeus* in order to make consistent the two pictures of the soul. First, I will show that the soul of the *Phaedo* is consistent with the immortal soul of the *Timaeus*. Second, I will argue that the *Phaedo* itself is speaking of the immortal soul. Plato has not just developed a three-part psychology in *Timaeus*. The full *Timaeus* psychology is not found in *Phaedo* explicitly, but may be found implicitly.

The *Phaedo* makes six claims about the soul. In order for the arguments against the death of the soul to work,[10] each of these descriptions must hold true. Do these descriptions fit within the cosmogony of the *Timaeus*? Does the reader encounter basic consistency between the soul of the *Phaedo* and that of *Timaeus*? She will, if she assumes that the soul of the *Phaedo* is the immortal soul of the *Timaeus*. I will argue briefly for the wisdom of that assumption later.[11]

First, the *Phaedo* claims that the human soul is "most like the divine." Can this claim be held within the world view of the *Timaeus*? It can be. In fact, it is necessary within that world view. The Father/Creator personally creates the divine soul element, which has existence apart from the body. This element communicates with and learns from the Father before its incarnation. The lesser gods create the human body and place the soul within it. It is a mistake to read the *Timaeus* as making the human body necessary to the existence of the immortal part of the human soul. Souls require body, but that need not be a human body. Souls exist and can think on their star before incarnation.[12] Human souls are, therefore, always incarnate, but not always in human bodies.

The divine soul of *Timaeus* does fit the *Phaedo*'s definition of being "most like the divine." The soul, without the human body, shares the motion of the Same in its astral body. The divine soul is created by the Father and the human body and mortal soul only by the lesser gods. There is no conflict between the description of the *Phaedo* and the cosmogony of the *Timaeus* at this point.

Second, the *Phaedo* describes the soul as deathless. Does the

Timaeus support this? If by death one means physical death, then there is no problem. Despite the fact that it is enmeshed in the body, the divine soul undergoes many births in the universe of the *Timaeus*. "And anyone who lived well for his appointed time would return home to his native star and live an appropriately happy life; but anyone who failed to do so would be changed ... at his ... birth."[13]

Thirdly, the *Phaedo* pictures the soul as being intelligible. What does Plato mean when he says that the soul is intelligible? Does it mean that humans can comprehend the nature of the soul, or that the soul is capable of exercising intelligence? Under either way of understanding the passage, there is no contradiction between the *Timaeus* and the *Phaedo*. Timaeus, the person telling the story of the formation of the soul, is human. He knows something about the divine soul, so the divine soul in the *Timaeus* is at least partially intelligible. Since he relates a story about the divine soul before its incarnation, it is clear that the *Timaeus* divine soul is knowable without a body.

Is the soul capable of exercising intelligence without a body? Timaeus, in his account of the pre-incarnate soul, says that each soul is shown, "the nature of the universe ... and the laws of ... destiny."[14] The God does this to avoid any responsibility for later evil actions by the incarnate souls. The pre-incarnate soul is able to exercise intelligence.

Fourth, the soul of the *Phaedo* is described as uniform. If one understands uniform as meaning "made only of one substance," then there is a problem with the mixing of the divine soul by the Creator/Father pictured in the *Timaeus*. Is there a way of understanding uniform to allow for the mixing process pictured in the formation of the divine soul in the *Timaeus*? Uniform might mean that the divine soul has internal consistency. Within the mixture of the *Timaeus* divine soul there is no division or irregularities. All the parts of the divine soul are evenly composed of all the components that go into the production of the divine soul.

Fifth, the soul is indissoluble. This seems to present a problem. Even the gods of the *Timaeus* are not indissoluble. The passage cited earlier in the paper makes it clear that anything bonded potentially could be destroyed by the Father/Creator. The solution to this apparent conflict is to understand the two Platonic uses of the word "indissoluble." The first usage refers to something, like the Father/Creator, that is necessarily indissoluble. There is no possible world where this object could be dissolved.

Then there are objects that are possibly dissoluble but are practically indissoluble. Human divine souls are in this category. Because they are good, there is no rational cause for their ever being destroyed. Since only the Creator could destroy them, and since He could never have cause to destroy them, they will never be destroyed in the actual world. They are not indissoluble in the strict sense because one could imagine a possible world where human divine souls were not good. This would be a world where Necessity thwarted the plans of the Creator to a much greater extent than was tolerable to him. In this world, humans souls would be destroyed by the Creator.

Plato uses only one term for both strictly indissoluble things and accidentally indissoluble things, because in practice, in the actual Platonic world, there is no difference between the two of them. The human divine soul of the *Phaedo* is indissoluble in the weak sense of that word.

The sixth description applied to the soul in the *Phaedo* is that the soul is always the same. What does Plato mean by an object being "always the same"? The solution is similar to the one proposed for the last attribute. It would seem that there is a weak view of "changelessness" and a strong view. An object may be "always the same" by never gaining or losing any attributes. This strong view of changelessness is certainly not possible for the divine soul of the *Timaeus*. It can be confused by placement within the body.

A weak view of "always the same" might deal with essential nature. A person might look at older woman and say, "She is just the same as when I first knew her fifty years ago." What does a person mean by this? It certainly would not mean that the woman had not changed in any of her attributes. It would seem to mean that some fundamental essence of who the woman was had not changed. The expression "always being the same" can be used in a weak sense to mean a consistency of fundamental attributes. This in fact must be what Socrates means when he speaks of the divine soul in the *Phaedo*. The divine soul is deathless. At the moment of the *Phaedo* discourse, one attribute of the divine soul of Socrates is that it is embodied. Soon the soul of Socrates would lose this property, as Socrates well knew, but he still believed that his soul was unchanging. Therefore, he must have believed in some weak form of changelessness along the lines I have suggested.

Is the soul of the *Timaeus* unchanging in this weak sense? The divine soul of the *Timaeus* may be confused, it may miss the mark, but its nature never changes. In the process of reincarnation, it remains capable of providing a source of movement to a body. Each soul retains its essential "soulishness."

The description of the soul in the *Phaedo* can be made consistent with the immortal soul of the *Timaeus*. Why assume that Plato is choosing between *Timaeus'* psychological elements? Why not just assume that Plato's psychology has become richer from the earlier *Phaedo* to the later *Timaeus*? Development in the Platonic psychology from the *Phaedo* to the *Timaeus* would not be fatal to my thesis. The *Phaedo* psychology, which is the earlier of the two, would simply be incomplete in comparison to the richer description found in the *Timaeus*. The *Timaeus* would still be the key to understanding the Platonic psychology. I believe, however, that there is an implicit indication in the text that the soul of the *Phaedo* is the immortal soul element of the *Timaeus*.

First, it is important to recall that the central focus of the *Phaedo* is the deathless soul, not psychology per se. Plato is showing that some part of Socrates will survive death. There is, therefore, no reason for the dialogue to delve into the mortal soul. This portion of the psychology will not provide comfort to the disciples of Socrates and it is not relevant to discussions of immortality. In short, the fact that it is not explicitly mentioned is not surprising.

At *Phaedo* 94d Socrates says,

> Well then, do we not now find that the soul acts in exactly the opposite way, leading those elements of which it is said to consist and opposing them (feelings of the body) in almost everything through all our life, and tyrannizing over them in every way, sometimes inflicting harsh and painful punishments (those of gymnastics and medicine), and sometimes milder ones, sometimes threatening and some times admonishing, in short speaking to the desires and passions and fears as if it were distinct from them and they from it.

Plato in this passage has made "desires and passions, and fears" a part of the body.

Did Plato intend to put these conscious states within the body?[15] This is difficult to believe. As David Gallop   points out, "Pleasure and pain are viewed (by Plato) not merely as changes in the body, but as psychic states (*Philebus* 33d2-e1, 35c3-d7, 55b3)."

On a simplistic reading of the text, Plato has simply been inconsistent with later dialogues. Is it not more likely that Plato has simply chosen to conflate the mortal soul of *Timaeus*, which would be the seat of passions, with the body in *Phaedo*? Why would he do this? The features of the mortal soul significant to the *Phaedo* make it more like the body than the immortal soul. The body and mortal soul are both things that die. They are, therefore, alike from the perspective of the argument for the immortality of some part of the human. I have already suggested that mortal soul is a bridge between the body and the immortal soul in the *Timaeus*. In *Timaeus,* Plato chose to place emphasis on the features of the mortal soul that make it "soulish." In the *Phaedo*, his focus is fixed on dying and not dying. This focus makes the mortal soul more like the body than the immortal soul.

The text itself places some distance between the body and these conscious states of desires, passions, and fears. Using a quotation from Homer's Odyssey, Plato relates this seat of passion to the "heart."[16] The heart with its passions is made distinct from the soul.

The heart is made part of the body, for Plato's purposes. Yet καρδία (heart) is used by Homer in the Odyssey itself at 4.572 to refer to mind.[17] Plato has picked a word that has a   double meaning. It can refer to a part of the body or it can refer to mind. This at least suggests that Plato has the mortal soul in mind. When he turns to the function of the heart, he then affirms its status as part of the human soul. Plato has, therefore, used soul in the *Phaedo* in a manner consistent with the *Timaeus* and in a way that at least suggests that he is referring only to the immortal soul of *Timaeus*.

Light from the *Timaeus* on the Psychology of the *Phaedo*

There are four basic arguments in the *Phaedo* for the immortality of the soul. It will not be my purpose to argue for the immortality of the soul or defend any of these arguments in detail. I simply wish to show that if one assumes that Plato is in fact using the full psychology found in *Timaeus*, then a strong criticism of one these arguments can be refuted. The argument that I will defend is Plato's "Argument from Cycles" at *Phaedo* 69e-72d. In defending this argument, I will make use of the terminology of an excellent summary of the argument found in Bostock's book, *Plato's Phaedo*.[18]

Plato's first argument for the immortality of the soul is based on opposition and cycles.[19] In this argument, Socrates claims that all living things come from their opposite: dead things. Since some things are alive, there must be a process to bring life from death. I am not trying to defend the "Cyclical Argument" from all possible assaults. I will, however, show that one important claim of the argument has been misunderstood and that this misunderstanding rests on a failure to account for the psychology and cosmology found in *Timaeus*.[20]

David Bostock's attack on the argument centers on the Platonic idea that life and death are opposites. Bostock describes the second premise of the cyclical argument as: "ii. Being alive has an opposite, namely being dead."[21] Bostock comments,

> The most obvious fault with this argument is that its second premise is false. We have noted that if the first premise is to be true, then the relevant kind of opposites must be properties that are contradictories of one another, and the properties of being alive and being dead are not contradictories: some things are neither alive nor dead. At least, this is certainly so if part of what is meant by saying that a thing is dead is that it used to be alive. For example a stone is not alive, and is not in this sense dead either, since it never was alive. More importantly to the argument, something that does not yet exist at all (for example my first grandchild) is not now either alive or dead.[22]

Bostock has launched a strong assault on the cyclical argument. The force of the assault depends on his understanding of "dead" and "alive." He argues with apparent justification that some things are neither dead nor alive: rocks and his future grandchild. Is this, however, true for Plato? Bostock says that one would have to believe that everything that is dead used to be alive.[23] Is that true?

The second point is not true, even on Bostock's account of the argument. Bostock's statement is based on an application of Plato's theory of opposites which Bostock renders as: "If anything x comes to be P (have any property), and if being P has an opposite, then x comes to be P from being the opposite of P."[24] Using this axiom, Bostock should not have asked if everything that is dead used to be alive, but if everything that comes to be dead used to be alive.

This is a critical difference. It means that if "x" is dead and has been eternally dead,[25] that it does not have to come from the living to be dead. It is only gaining or losing properties that are covered by the principle, not keeping them. Can Plato sensibly assert that everything that (1) comes to be dead used to be alive, and (2) comes to be alive used to be dead? I believe that he can and does in *Timaeus*.

The cosmology of *Timaeus*, quite different from that of Bostock, explains how Plato could make such a seemingly obvious error. If one accepts the cosmology and psychology of the *Timaeus*, then everything that comes to be dead, did indeed used to be alive, and everything that is alive did indeed used to dead. This includes the rocks, and Bostock's future grandchild.

In *Timaeus* one discovers that at death, soul and body go their own ways. Dying is losing the soul. Socrates' body will lose its immortal soul and perhaps even its mortal soul. To be dead, then, is at least to have no rational motion from the immortal human soul. The dead human being ceases to be involved in any rational motion, because it has not rational soul. The living human being, on the other hand, has the rational human soul and at least some rational motion, however warped and impeded it might be.[26] Dead things are contradictories of living things. Dead things are all those things which have no rational motion.[27] Living things are those things that have such a rational motion. The cosmic animal is declared alive for just this cause.[28] In short:

> Definition 1: Cosmologically, all living things do have some form of circular motion.
>
> Definition 2: Cosmologically, all dead things do not have some form of circular motion.

A thing either has circular motion or it does not.

Bostock's examples are, therefore, failures. The rock is dead in the Platonic sense. It has no rational and circular motions.[29] Bostock's grandchild, if the full cosmological account is taken into account, is alive. She or he has at present a circular motion on its star or is present in a body. Of course, one must not answer the question in this manner since immortality itself is the issue of the *Phaedo* argument. Without begging the question then, if Bostock's grandchild were to come to life, then it would do so from the dead. The elements that would make up the soul of young Bostock (Same, Different, and Being) have no motion before the soul is created. The elements of the body

(Fire, Air, Water, and Earth) are not moving in a circle just before they are used to create a body.[30]

The rock example yields further clarification. The rock is now dead. It lacks circular motion. Bostock would have the reader ask, "Was the rock ever alive?" Bostock assumes that the rock as rock was never alive. This, he believes, contradicts the first premise of the cyclical argument. I have already shown, however, that it does not. The cyclical argument only deals with things that take on the property of being dead, not things that have that property for their entire existence. This is true on Bostock's own account of the argument.

The text of the *Phaedo* supports Bostock's reading, "Let us see with regard to all these (living things), whether it is true that they are all born or generated only from their opposites."[31] We have seen that Bostock formulated this notion more broadly as a thing "coming to have a property." Plato is talking only about things that have properties as a result of generation. I have shown that it is sensible to say that Bostock's rock is dead. It either has always been dead or was once part of a body. If it came to be dead, then it did so from an object with rational motion. In other words, it lost circular motion.

All of this supports the Platonic argument. If it always has been dead, or more precisely if the geometric particles that make it have always failed to have rational motions, then it has not "come to have the property death." It never died, or lost rational motions, it is simply dead. Bostock has confused Platonic dying and generation with being alive and being dead. If Plato takes his own definitions into account, or at least definitions to which he came in later life, he can save the cyclical argument from this particular attack. The argument may fail on other grounds, as I believe it does, but not because of this "obvious fault" in Plato's argument.

It does not seem that there is any real conflict between the soul of the *Timaeus* and the soul of the *Phaedo*. The two pictures can be made consistent. The psychology I have found in the *Timaeus* has saved one of the arguments for immortality in the *Phaedo* from a forceful objection. What of the soul described in the *Republic*?

The Soul of the City: The Psychology of the *Republic*

The *Republic's* and the *Timaeus'* Psychology: Do They Compliment Each Other?

The psychology of the *Republic* is much like that found in *Timaeus*. The issue to be examined in comparing the psychology of the two dialogues is to what extent the two descriptions of a tripartite soul compliment each other.

The *Republic* seeks to establish that the just person is the happiest person. It does this by examining the functioning of the ideal state. By looking at the just actions of humanity as a group in a polis, Plato, through the voice of Socrates, hopes to be able to discern what justice would be in the individual. Plato's ideal state ends up containing three classes of citizens: the guardians, the auxiliaries, and the common laborer. Justice in the ideal city is defined as, "... the possession of one's own and the performance of one's own task ...."[32]

Plato believes that there are three parallel parts to the human soul.[33] He argues that there must be three separate parts of the human soul in order to explain psychological conflict. These three parts are: the rational, the spirited, and the appetitive.[34]

The rational part of the soul is in command of the just person. Plato describes it as "being wise and exercising foresight on behalf of the whole soul."[35] The rational part of the soul performs the function of the guardian in the *Republic*. It helps maintain the appropriate balance within the parts of the human body and mind.

The spirited part of the soul acts as the servant of the rational part in the just person. It aids the soul by "fighting, following its leader (the rational part), and by its courage fulfilling his decisions."[36]

What of the third part of the soul? The third part of the soul is the location of "the pleasures of food and procreation."[37] These pleasures are to be firmly under the control of the other two parts of the soul. The human who does not have control over his or her physical desires is considered the worst sort of human in the *Republic*.

The relationship between the accounts of the soul in the *Phaedo*, *Timaeus*, and the *Republic* is clear. The tripartite soul of the *Republic* is the divine soul element and the mortal soul element of the *Timaeus* with both parts of the mortal soul being counted as separate in the *Republic* account.

What is the evidence for this view? First, the divine soul

element is the seat of intellectual virtues in *Timaeus*.[38] This corresponds
to the first part of the "tripartite" soul of the *Republic*.[39] The reasonable
part of the soul should be in charge of the entire soul in each of the
dialogues. As *Timaeus* says of the immortal soul, "... it (is) the most
divine part ... reigning over all the parts within us."[40] The *Republic* is
just as clear, "Does it not belong to the rational part to rule?
'Assuredly.'"[41] In the myth of Er   found at the conclusion of the
Republic, Plato says that a human soul after death can only be saved by
the knowledge it has gained in its mortal life.[42] Plato states in the
Republic that the Good Itself is grasped by the intellectual part of the
soul.[43] In the tripartite soul he has described in the   *Republic*, both the
function of ruling the body and of gaining knowledge should only be
given to the first part of the tripartite soul. As we have seen, these
functions are equivalent to those described for the divine element of the
Phaedo and *Timaeus*.

The most important function of the soul is to grasp the good
itself. The "recollectable" knowledge of the Forms and the Good is
surely the "most divine" ability given to the soul. Plato reserves this
ability for the first part of the tripartite soul. The first part of the
tripartite soul of the *Republic* and the divine soul element of the other
two dialogues should be viewed as being descriptions of the same soul
part.

The second and third part of the souls are just as surely the
two parts of the mortal soul described in the *Timaeus*.[44] The spirited
part of the soul in the *Republic* is to help the reasoned part rule the soul.
It is to function as an auxiliary to help guard the soul against evil.[45] We
have already seen that this is the exact function of the heart area in the
mortal soul element pictured in the *Timaeus*.[46] Similar attributes, like
courage, are attributed to the spirited part and the heart area of the
mortal soul. *Timaeus* says of it, "... that part of the soul which partakes
of courage and spirit . . ."[47] *Republic* agrees, "... the other giving battle,
attending upon the ruler, and by its courage executing the ruler's
design."[48]

There is no reason not to view them as equivalent. In the myth
of Er, persons make their choices based on reason and knowledge, or
the lack thereof, not on their courage or other heart virtue.[49] There is no
strong evidence in the *Republic* for this second part of the tripartite soul
functioning after death. There is no reason to deny its equivalence to
the heart section of the mortal soul of the *Timaeus*.

According to the *Republic*, the worst state of affairs in a human life comes to pass when the part of the soul devoted to appetite rules.[50] This is exactly what Plato implies in the *Timaeus* for the belly section of the mortal soul.[51] The *Republic* describes the third section of the human soul as dealing with the appetite for food.[52] The *Timaeus* describes the belly part of the mortal soul element as being concerned with food.[53] The third part of the *Republic*'s description of soul is the belly section of the mortal soul element of the *Timaeus*.

The chief problem is reconciling the tripartite soul of the *Republic* with the elements of the soul in the *Timaeus* and *Phaedo*. Why does Plato not simply use his description of the soul-system in the *Timaeus*? Why does he separate the two regions of the mortal soul element?

The answer to these questions lies in the purpose of the *Republic*. The goal of the *Republic* is to find the answer to the questions, "What is justice? Is the just person the most happy person?" Plato's description of the soul is from an ethical and political point of view in order to answer these questions. Plato wants to describe both the just and the properly governed soul.

The *Republic* is not concerned with questions of origins or physical location of the soul elements. These are the very features of the belly region and the heart region which make them part of one mortal soul element. A description of the relationship between the two parts of the mortal soul element is not an important task in the *Republic*. It is the separate ethical and political roles of these soul parts that he wishes to utilize, not their biological and cosmological functional unity.[54]

The ethical and political dimensions of the Plato's psychology are not the major concerns of the other two dialogues. The *Phaedo* desires to establish the immortality of the soul and so deals only with the divine element. The goal of the *Timaeus* is to present a history of the origin of the soul and to picture a functioning soul in a body. The *Timaeus* agrees with the dissection of the soul in terms of its constitutive physical parts. It then gives a physical description of the functioning of those parts in the body. The *Republic* needs parts for the soul but is not concerned with the function of the parts except in so far as they effect the governance and ethical status of the soul.

In the *Timaeus,* a relationship between the heart region of the mortal soul and the divine soul element is suggested. The heart region helps control the belly region for the divine soul. This is not the relationship that the *Timaeus* focuses on. The heart region also is closely related to the belly region. Both parts of these two regions of the soul are mortal, both were created by the demigods and not the Father/Creator, and both parts are located in the trunk of a human. For the cosmological and biological concerns of the *Timaeus,* this second relationship is that one that is emphasized.

The Human Soul in the City Revealed in the Cosmology of the *Timaeus*

The psychology of the *Timaeus* ties in remarkably well with the message of *Republic*. If one reads them together, both serve to illuminate the arguments of the other. If one begins with the psychology of the *Timaeus*, then portions of the *Republic* become much more clear. A wonderful harmony emerges from close study of the two dialogues. One example will suffice to show the potential power of the *Timaeus* psychology in clearing up difficulties in the *Republic's* account of the soul.

At *Republic* 441a-c, Plato distinguishes between the "spirited soul" and the "rational soul." He says that the spirited soul "marshals itself on the side of reason."[55] Using a quot ation from Homer, he points out that at times human intellect must restrain the high-spiritedness of reason.[56]

This account of the relationship between the spirited soul and the rational soul in the *Republic* has caused difficulties for some commentators. In his cogent work, *A Companion to Plato's Republic,* Nicholas White says,

> It is not entirely clear just what Plato thinks occurs when reason advises and exhorts spirit. Are we to think of spirit as in some way understanding the thoughts or words of reason? To do so might threaten to assign a kind of rationality, of a kind that Plato might intend to attribute to the reasoning soul alone.[57]

This is a real worry. White points out that later, in *Republic,* Plato again speaks of the rational soul "retaining the declarations of reason."[58] Plato speaks of "all the parts of the soul sharing a common belief concerning who should rule" at 432a8.[59] White concedes that some of this language must be taken as loose or figurative, but he still is at a loss to know what to make of it.

The psychology of the *Timaeus* resolves such worries. The goal of the *Republic* is to show that the rational soul can control the powerful emotions of the spirited soul. These emotions can then be turned to helping maintain the rational soul's rule. However, the rational soul has only been described in intellectual terms in the earlier *Phaedo*. *Republic* is, therefore, limited to intellectual descriptions of the immortal soul's activity in dealing with the middle soul.

The *Timaeus* also ascribes the intellectual function to the rational soul, but it tells how that intellectual function works and describes its physical home. As we have seen, the rational soul of the *Timaeus* is self-moving with a natural circular motion. In the human, it is lodged in the head and directly impacts the brain-marrow. Intellectual activity is thereby associated with a physical phenomenon.

How does this account in *Timaeus* solve the problem presented by White? The text makes clear the relationship between the two soul parts at *Timaeus* 70a,

> That part of the soul, then, which partakes of courage and spirit, since it is a lover of victory, they planted more near to the head, between the midriff and the neck, in order that it might hearken to the reason, and, in conjunction therewith, might forcibly subdue the tribe of the desires whensoever they should utterly refuse to yield obedience to the word of command from the citadel of reason.

The heart is the major organ of that region and it is

> ... the chamber of the bodyguard, to the end that when the heat of passion boils up, as soon as reason passes the word round that some unjust action is being done which affects them, either from without or possibly even from interior desires, every organ of sense in the body might quickly perceive through all the channels both the injunctions and the threats and in all ways obey and follow them, thus allowing their best part to be the leader of them all.[60]

How can these passages be understood in the light of the psychology presented earlier? What does it mean for the mortal soul to "hearken?" I agree with White that it would be of great concern if Plato, in fact, had reasoning taking place in any area apart from the rational soul. The physical account in *Timaeus* of the immortal soul's reasoning removes this danger. The immortal soul, in its ideal state, moves in the circular motions of Reason. In a less than ideal human, the immortal soul would still move at times in motions fairly close to the circles. These motions are, as I have demonstrated, the source for reason in the human.[61] The mortal soul provides non-rational motion for things like digestion or heart motion in the lower body.[62]

The rational motion interacts with the lower mortal soul through the neck.[63] This allows some contact, but keeps the immortal soul from being overwhelmed. The purpose of the warnings or instructions to the heart region is made clear in the text at 70d. The heart and the blood system acts as the carrier of instructions to the rest of the body. What are these instructions? Based on my earlier arguments, they are impulses to motion from the immortal soul. These impulses strengthen the proper motions of the mortal soul and enable it to perform all of its functions. For example, immortal soul could send motions to the soul/body complex in the stomach to counteract an evil motion that was impeding the work of digestion.

The circular motion of the immortal soul is transmitted through the neck. How does this work? One can take the details provided from the text and suggest an image of how such a system might work. Plato himself does not give the details. He simply pictures the immortal soul transmitting "instructions" and "warnings." It is possible, however, to take the facts that are given and extrapolate to how Plato might have conceived this system as working.

The circles of the immortal soul would be in contact with the motions of the mortal soul in the neck through the marrow.[64] The neck is thin and so the immortal soul is in contact with a relatively small amount of mortal soul encased in neck marrow.[65] In a well-ordered human, the motion of the immortal soul in the head would command or be stronger than the motions of the mortal soul in the marrow of the neck region. Mortal soul, which can move in any of five directions as appropriate,[66] can be "pushed" in the appropriate direction by the ever-circling brain marrow.

Neck marrow with its mortal soul does not itself move in a circle. It cannot or it would itself be rational.[67] How can the immortal soul move the mortal soul? Plato does not say clearly, but given what is known, it must work in something like the following manner.

An object that is moving in a circle that hits another object in motion will tend to knock it off in another direction. If the immortal soul wishes to send a direction to the mortal soul, it need only hit the mortal soul in the appropriate manner. The direction the mortal soul/neck marrow takes will depend on the angle at which the spinning motion of the mortal soul makes contact with it. The immortal soul can hit the neck marrow by increasing in size at the right moment to catch the moving neck marrow at the right angle.[68] The neck marrow can then pass on this new motion by making contact with other marrow, and from there to blood, leading all the way to the heart. The heart then transmits this motion to the entire soul/body complex. Of course, the interaction of motions would be very complex.

The *Timaeus* reports that the immortal soul sends warnings to the heart. These warnings are not "intellectual." It is not as if the immortal soul is sending a set of propositions to the chest region. There is a way of at least picturing this warning at a physical level that keeps rational motion in the head.

The brain could warn the heart, and hence the body, in the manner I have just briefly described. The brain might have some memory of a particular motion. In a well-ordered human, this memory would involve being attracted by the approach of a similar good motion in matter or being repulsed by a dissimilar motion in matter. Memory, it should be recalled, was earlier described as just such a strengthening of proper movement and a weakening of contrary motions. These strengthened motions produce a group of attractions and repulsions in the immortal soul/brain complex that enable warnings to be sent to the rest of the body.

Let me give a simple example. The immortal soul might receive contrary motions through the marrow from the body. This would indicate that the body was undergoing some assault of improper motions from either outside or within itself.[69] It could then moderate the motion of the soul/body by sending a harmonizing motion. The heart would pass this motion on throughout the body. Then the body, being given improper rightward motion in its hands, could send a counter-balancing leftward motion through the neck and the circulatory system, to the hands.

This at least shows that one need not be concerned about the spirited soul of the *Republic* being a reasoning part. *Timaeus'* psychology gives the broad outlines of a psychic system of motions allowing for warnings from the immortal soul and exhortations from the spirited soul without intelligence being placed in the mortal soul.

While some of this picture is speculative, it closely tied to the data presented in the text.

It is certain that the psychology of the *Timaeus* and the *Republic* are consistent. I have also shown that the *Timaeus* gives the philosopher a problem-solving strategy that enables progress to be made in understanding an uncertain text in the *Republic*. My thesis is, therefore, confirmed once again.

Concluding Remarks

Just as the ideal city made plain the political aspects of the soul of the ideal human in *Republic*, so the most likely cosmology has presented us with the very essence of the human soul in *Timaeus*. The exegetical assumptions of the strong and weak-myth Platonists have caused them to miss this illuminating psychology.

What is that psychology? Plato has developed the early Greek notion of soul as motion. For Plato, soul is circular motion. This motion is rational and orderly. Plato has thereby made "soul" the seat of human intellectual activity and passion. By making the soul tripartite, he has allowed for psychological conflict in humans.

This soul contains three elements found in the head, the chest, and the belly. The rational soul of the head is immortal. The immortal soul has an accidental Form of simplicity not shared by the other two mortal elements. This immortal soul will appear to be first in birth and priority, though in fact there is no first moment of creation. The immortal soul is always found in a body. It is sometimes in an astral body, where its motion is natural. At other times, it is incarnate in the confusing sub-lunar world. There its motions are disturbed. It can no longer move in perfect circular motion. Only decreasing its contact with confusing motions and improper matter, while increasing its contact with proper motions and matter, can restore it to proper function.

The mortal soul, itself divided in two, acts as a bridge between the immortal soul and the human body. Plato has developed a naturalistic account of the relationships between the two types of soul and body. He need not resort to myth or religious language to describe the impact of the soul on the human body.

The human soul can only be ultimately individuated by its history and location. The soul of any given person is like the soul of any other given person living at the same time in terms of its composition and function. At the moment of death, the immortal soul is the only part that is sure to survive. Much of what is called personality will not necessarily survive the process. Only the rational parts of the human exist eternally.

This psychology can form the basis for predictions about the visible world. For example, Plato would predict that there are more animals than humans, if his full psychology is true. Since Plato does not believe the visible world to be real in the strong sense, it cannot be shown to be false. It can, however, be found more or less plausible. Plato's psychology, therefore, is not inconsistent with some scientific examination of the world.

Plato is not a substance dualist. For Plato, only the Forms are real. The visible world is only a becoming thing. The human being is composed of two parts: body and soul. Neither of these two parts are real, both are becoming things. Humans are, therefore, composed of only one sort of thing. On the other hand, soul and body are two irreducible categories of becoming. There is a weak sense, therefore, in which Plato has a dualistic view of humanity.

This psychology also allows for some divination. This divination need not be understood in a religious manner, but as an alternative method for the orderly nature of the Forms to impact the immortal soul. The immortal soul usually finds order by looking outside itself. The divination of the liver allows for an ordering that comes from within the body and mortal soul of the human.

The psychology of the *Timaeus* is consistent with that of *Phaedo*. The immortal soul of the *Timaeus* is quite compatible with the soul of the *Phaedo*. There is a good textual reason for thinking that such a correspondence is not foreign to the *Phaedo* itself. Of course, the *Timaeus* could be a development of the *Phaedo,* making the whole soul of the *Phaedo* a mere part of the whole soul of *Timaeus*. In any case, the *Timaeus* psychology allows for a more charitable understanding of the argument for immortality based on cycles. Plato's argument is thereby saved from a strong criticism.

The psychology of the *Republic* is illuminated by the psychology found in *Timaeus*. The richer and more precise account found in *Timaeus* helps clarify a difficult passage in the *Republic*. The *Timaeus* has been shown to contain Plato's best psychological views. The *Timaeus* is the key to the Platonic psychology.

[1] Gerson, Lloyd. "A Note on Tripartition and Immortality in Plato" in *Apeiron: a Journal for Ancient Philosophy and Science*, 1987, 81-95.

[2] *Phaedo* 78c.

[3] Gerson, note 1 on page 81.

[4] There are other problems of consistency within the Platonic psychology. Gerson lists and deals with several putative problems within the Platonic psychology found in several dialogues. It is not my purpose to deal with the particular discrepancy between the account in *Phaedrus* and the other dialogues that Gerson focuses on and then handles with some skill.

[5] My work in the *Republic* was based on a two year study session in the Greek text of that dialogue with Professor Al Geier of the University of Rochester. I am grateful for his input in this section.

[6] Plato, *Five Dialogues* translated by G.M.A. Grube (Indianapolis: Hackett Publishing Company, 1981), 89.

[7] I will assume that the work is a fiction on the part of Plato around the actual event of the death of Socrates. On the other hand, nothing I will say would be disturbed if the opinions expressed in the dialogue were also those of Socrates. On either reading, the reader is confronted with Plato's longest written set of arguments regarding the immortality of the soul.

[8] *Phaedo* 69e.

[9] *Phaedo* 80b.

[10] I am not implying they would "work" for anyone. But if all the attributes hold for the immortal soul of *Timaeus*, then Plato, who made the *Phaedo* arguments hinge on the soul having these attributes, would have thought that they worked. In fact, I find all the arguments unconvincing.

[11] It is not conclusive that Plato uses "soul" without qualification in the *Phaedo*. Plato uses "soul" (without qualification) to refer to parts of the soul in *Timaeus*. See for example: 41e where the immortal part is simply "soul" and 70e where the mortal soul is "soul" and 72d where the soul-system is called "soul" without qualification.

[12] *Timaeus* 41.

[13] *Timaeus* 42-43.

[14] *Timaeus* 41.

[15] Gallop, David. *Plato's* Phaedo. (Oxford: Oxford University Press, 1980), 89.

[16] *Phaedo* 94d.

[17] This meaning appears in the full citation for kardiva found in Liddell and Scott. *Greek English Lexicon*, 9th ed. (1990), s.v. "kardiva" I.3.

[18] Bostock, David. (Oxford: Oxford University Press, 1986.)

[19] *Phaedo* 69e-72d.

[20] Bostock, 42-59.

[21] Bostock, 51.

[22] Bostock, 52.

[23] This is based on Plato's own notion that everything that comes to be, comes

to be from its opposite. I would not want to defend that notion!

[24] Bostock, 51.

[25] On a creationist account of *Timaeus*, "dead from creation."

[26] The *Timaeus* says nothing about humans who are incapable of reason. I see no reason from the text to think that if Plato recognized that utterly irrational persons were possible, that he would have continued to call them "living." It is important to remember that "reason" was a claim about motion; animals have a rational soul, so that Plato was not saying one had to do high-level thinking in order to demonstrate possession of the rational motions.

[27] *Timaeus* 88a makes it clear that the living creature is just the compound of soul and body.

[28] See *Timaeus* 37d where the Demiurge gives the cosmic animal circular motion, sees it moving, and is delighted in its life.

[29] Of course, Bostock could be talking about a moon rock, in which case it is alive!

[30] Of course it is possible that the elements of the body of Bostock Jr. are in my body at present, and will someday be in his body. In that case, they are now alive, will be dead, and then come to life again. Before they were in my body, they were dead. This is exactly what Plato meant in his argument.

[31] *Phaedo* 70e.

[32] *Republic* 433b (Grube).

[33] He reaches this conclusion by an analogy with the ideal city.

[34] *Republic* 440-444.

[35] *Republic* 441.

[36] *Republic* 442b.

[37] *Republic* 436b.

[38] *Timaeus* 37a-d.

[39] *Republic* 441e.

[40] *Timaeus* 44.

[41] *Republic* 441e.

[42] *Republic* 617c-e.

[43] *Republic* 532b.

[44] *Timaeus* 69d-72d.

[45] *Republic* 442b.

[46] *Timaeus* 70a.

[47] *Timaeus* 70a4.

[48] *Republic* 442b.

[49] *Republic* 617d and following.

[50] See *Republic* Book IX, particularly 582 and following.

[51] *Timaeus* 70.

[52] *Republic* 437b.

[53] *Timaeus* 70e.

[54] In other words, the mortal soul element achieves its unity through: 1.

common cosmological parent for each of its parts, 2. common biological function, self-generated motion, 3.common physical location, the trunk, and 4. common mortality. None of these attributes is important for the project of the *Republic* and so the mortal soul element is not mentioned in the *Republic*.

[55] *Republic* 440e.

[56] *Republic* 441c.

[57] White, Nicholas P. *A Companion to Plato's* Republic (Indianapolis: Hackett Publishing, 1979), 126.

[58] White, 129. *Republic* 442c2.

[59] White, 129.

[60] *Timaeus* 70d.

[61] *Timaeus* 42d.

[62] *Timaeus* 70a and following.

[63] *Timaeus* 69e.

[64] *Timaeus* 70d.

[65] *Timaeus* 69e makes it clear that this was the very purpose for creating the narrow neck "isthmus."

[66] This is inferred from the many jobs, like digestion and circulation, given to the mortal soul in *Timaeus* 70-72e. Without all five motions, the mortal soul would not be able to perform all of these functions.

[67] One can infer its non-circular motion from its name: mortal soul. If it were able to move in a circle, it would be able to reason. If it were able to reason, then it would be like the immortal soul.

[68] Can the immortal soul increase in size in order to do this? There is not text to say either way. This is, I think, reasonable speculation of what must be, if one is to make sense of the details Plato has given the reader. In other words, something like this must be true.

[69] *Timaeus* 70b.

Bibliography

Aquinas, Thomas. "Summa Theologica." In *Introduction to St. Thomas Aquinas*. Edited by Anton C. Pegis. New York: Modern Library, 1948.

Aristotle. *The Complete Works of Aristotle*. 2 vols. Edited by Jonathan Barnes. Princeton: Bollingen Series, 1984.

Aristotle. *De Anima*.

Aristotle. *On Generation and Corruption*.

Aristotle. *Physics*.

Augustine. *City of God*.

Bigger, Charles C. "On the World Soul in Plato's *Timaeus*." In *Southern Journal of Philosophy* (Spring, 1967), 1-8.

Bloom, Allan, trans. *The Republic,* by Plato. Translated with notes, interpretive essay, and a new introduction. New York: Harper Books, 1991.

Boardman, John; Griffin, Jasper; and Murray, Oswyn, Editors. *The Oxford History of the Classical World*. Oxford: Oxford University Press, 1986.

Bostock, David, trans. *Phaedo*, by Plato. Oxford: Oxford University Press, 1986.

Bremmer, Jan. *The Early Greek Concept of the Soul*. Princeton: Princeton University Press, 1983.

Brush, Stephen G. "Ghosts of the Nineteenth Century." In *Scientists Confront Creationism*. Edited by Laurie R. Godfrey. New York: Norton, 1983.

Burkert, Walter. *Greek Religion*. Cambridge: Harvard University Press, 1985.

Burnet, John. *Greek Philosophy*. New York: MacMillan, 1960.

Cherniss, H.F. "The Relation of the *Timaeus* to Plato's Later Dialogues." In *Studies in Plato's Metaphysics*. Edited by R.E. Allen. London: Routledge and Kegan Paul, 1965.

Copleston, Frederick. *A History of Philosophy*. Vol.1, *Greece and Rome*. New York: Image Books, 1989.

Cornford, F.M. *From Religion to Philosophy*. Princeton: Princeton University Press, 1991.

Cornford, F.M. *Plato's Cosmology*. London: Routledge and Kegan Paul, 1977.

Dawkins, Richard. *The Blind Watchmaker*. New York: W.W. Norton, 1987.

Dictionary of Philosophy. 1979 ed., s.v. "Charity Principle." Flew, Antony. St Martins Press, 1979.

Ficino, Marsilio. *Platonic Theology*. Cambridge: Harvard University Press, 2001.

Fox, Robin. *Pagans and Christians*. New York: Alfred A. Knopf, 1986.

Frost, Frank J. *Greek Society*. Lexington, Mass.: D.C. Heath and Company, 1971.

Gallop, David, trans. *Phaedo*. Oxford: Clarendon Press, 1980.

Gavin, William J. "Science and Myth in the *Timaeus*." In *Southwestern Journal of Philosophy*. (Summer, 1975), 7-15.

Geier, Alfred. *Plato's Erotic Thought*. Rochester: University of Rochester Press, 2002.

Gerson, Lloyd. "A Note on Tripartition and Immortality in Plato."

Apeiron (1987), 81-96.

Grant, Michael. *The Rise of the Greeks*. New York: Scribners, 1988.

Guthrie, Kenneth. *The Pythagorean Sourcebook and Library*. Grand Rapids: Phanes Press, 1987.

Gosse, Philip. *Omphalos: An Attempt to Untie the Geological Knot*. London: John Van Voorst, 1857.

Grote, George. *Plato and the Other Companions of Socrates*. London: John Murray, 1867.

Grube, G.M.A. *Plato's Thought*. Indianapolis: Hackett, 1980.

Havelock, Eric. *Preface to Plato*. Cambridge, Mass.: Harvard University Press, 1963.

Hippocrates. *On Ancient Medicine*. Translated by Francis Adams. In "Library of the Future: Third Edition" compact disk, World Library Inc., 1992.

Jowett, Benjamin. *Preface to the* Timaeus. New York: Liberal Arts Press, 1949.

Kirk, G.S., Raven, J.E., and Schoefield, M. *The Presocratic Philosophers*. Cambridge: Cambridge University Press, 1983.

Kraut, Richard. *The Cambridge Companion to Plato*. Cambridge: Cambridge University Press, 1992.

Lewis. C.S. *The Discarded Image*. Cambridge: Cambridge University Press, 1964; Canto Edition, 1994.

Long, A.A. and Sedley, D.N. *The Hellenistic Philosophers*. Vol 1. Cambridge: Cambridge University Press, 1988.

Mann, William E. "Simplicity and Immutability in God." In *The Concept of God*. Edited by Thomas V. Morris. Oxford: Oxford University Press, 1987.

McKirahan, Richard D. *Philosophy Before Socrates.* Indianapolis: Hackett, 1992.

Modrak, Deborah. *Aristotle: the Power of Perception.* Chicago: University of Chicago Press, 1989.

Morford, Mark P.O. and Lenardon, Robert. *Classical Mythology.* New York: Longman, 1991.

Nails, Debra. *The People of Plato.* Indianapolis: Hackett, 2002.

Owen, G.E.L. *Logic, Science, and the Dialectic.* Edited by Martha Nussbaum. Ithaca: Cornell University Press, 1986.

Owen, G.E.L. "The Place of the *Timaeus* in Plato's Dialogues." In *Studies in Plato's Metaphysics.* Edited by R.E. Allen. London: Routledge and Kegan Paul, 1965.

Pangle, Thomas. "Interpretive Essay." In *The* Laws *of Plato.* Translated by Thomas Pangle. Chicago: University of Chicago Press, 1988.

Pater, Walter. *Plato and Platonism.* New York: MacMillian Company, 1903.

Patterson, Richard. *Image and Reality in Plato's Metaphysics.* Indianapolis: Hackett, 1985.

Plato. *The Collected Dialogues.* Edited by Edith Hamilton and Huntington Cairns. Princeton: Princeton University Press, 1987.

Plato. *Critias.* Translated by R.G. Bury. Loeb Classical Library, no. 234. Cambridge, Mass: Harvard University Press, 1989.

Plato. *Cratylus.* Translated by B. Jowett. In "Library of the Future: Third Edition" compact disk, World Library Inc., 1992.

Plato. *Five Dialogues.* Translated by G.M.A. Grube. Indianapolis: Hackett Publishing Company, 1981.

Plato. *Meno*. Translated by W.R.M. Lamb. Loeb Classical Library, no. 167. Cambridge, Mass.: Harvard University Press, 1967.

Plato. *Parmenides* Translated by H.N. Fowler. Loeb Classical Library, no. 167. Cambridge, Mass.: Harvard University Press, 1977.

Plato. *Phaedrus*. Translated by H.N. Fowler. Loeb Classical Library, no. 167. Cambridge, Mass.: Harvard University Press, 1977.

Plato. *Laws*. Translated by R.G. Bury. Loeb Classical Library, nos. 187 and 192. Cambridge, Mass.: Harvard University Press, 1984

Plato *Laws*. Translated by Thomas L. Pangle. Chicago: University of Chicago Press, 1988.

Plato. *Lesser Hippias*. Translated by B. Jowett. In *The Collected Dialogues of Plato*. Edited by Edith Hamilton. Princeton: Princeton University Press, 1987.

Plato. *Phaedo*. Translated by H.N. Fowler. Loeb Classical Library, no. 36. Cambridge, Mass.: Harvard University Press, 1990.

Plato. *Platonis Opera*. 4 vols. Edited by John Burnet. Oxford: Oxford University Press.

Plato. *Republic*. Translated by Paul Shorey. Loeb Classical Library, nos. 237 and 276. Cambridge, Mass.: Harvard University Press, 1982.

Plato. *Symposium*. Translated by W.R.M. Lamb. Loeb Classical Library, no. 167. Cambridge, Mass.: Harvard University Press, 1967.

Plato. *Theatetus*. Translated by H. N. Fowler. Loeb Classical Library, no.32. Cambridge, Mass.: Harvard University Press, 1914.

Plato. *Timaeus*. Translated by R.G. Bury. Loeb Classical Library. Cambridge, Mass.: Harvard University Press, 1921.

Plato. *Timaeus*. Translated by B. Jowett. In "Library of the Future: Third Edition" compact disk, World Library Inc., 1992.

Plutarch. *Lives*. Translated by Bernadotte Perrin. Loeb Classical Library, no.32. Cambridge, Mass.: Harvard University Press, 1914.

Popper, Karl. *Popper Selections*. Edited by David Miller. Princeton: Princeton University Press, 1985.

Press, Gerald A. *Plato's Dialogues: New Studies and Interpretations*. Boston: Rowman and Littlefield, 1993.

Proclus. *Commentary on Plato's* Parmenides. Translated by Glenn R. Morrow and John M. Dillon. Princeton: Princeton University Press, 1987.

Proclus. *The Commentaries of Proclus on the* Timaeus *of Plato*. 2 vols. Translated by Thomas Taylor. Kila, Montana: Kessinger Publishing Company, 1995.

Puhvel, Jan. *Comparative Mythology*. Baltimore: Johns Hopkins University Press, 1987.

Robinson, T.M. *Plato's Psychology*. Unpublished paper given at Cornell University, Summer 1995.

Robinson, T.M. *Plato's Psychology*. Toronto: University of Toronto Press, 1970.

Ross, George MacDonald. "Angels." *Philosophy* (60, 1985), 495-511.

Runciman, W.G. "Plato's *Parmenides*." In *Studies in Plato's Metaphysics*. Edited by R.E. Allen. London: Routledge and Kegan Paul, 1965.

Ryle, Gilbert. "Plato's *Parmenides*." In *Studies in Plato's Metaphysics,* Edited by R.E. Allen. London: Routledge and Kegan Paul, 1965.

Sambursky, S. *The Physical World of the Greeks*. Princeton: Princeton University Press, 1987.

Sayre, Kenneth M. *Plato's Late Ontology: A Riddle Resolved*. Princeton: Princeton University Press, 1983.

Stewart, J.A. *The Myths of Plato.* Edited by G.R. Levy. Barnes and Noble, 1970.

Strauss, Leo. *The City and Man.* Chicago: University of Chicago Press, 1978.

Strauss, Leo. *Studies in Platonic Philosophy.* Chicago: University of Chicago Press, 1983.

Strauss, Leo. *Socrates and Aristophanes.* New York: Basic Books, 1966.

Strauss, Leo. *On Plato's Symposium.* Chicago: University of Chicago Press, 2001.

Sorabji, Richard. *Time, Creation, and the Continuum.* Ithaca: Cornell University Press, 1983.

Taylor, A.E. *Aristotle On His Predecessors.* Chicago: Open Court Publishing, 1927.

Taylor, A.E. *Commentary on Plato's* Timaeus. Oxford: Clarendon Press, 1928.

Taylor, A.E. *Plato.* New York: The Dial Press, 1927.

Tejera, V. *Plato's Dialogues One by One: A Structural Approach.* New York: Irvington Publishers, 1984.

Thilly, Frank. *A History of Philosophy.* Revised by Ledger Wood. New York: Holt, Rinehart, and Winston, 1961.

Van Inwagen, Peter. "Genesis and Evolution." In *Reasoned Faith.* Edited by Eleonore Stump. Cornell: Cornell University Press, 1993.

Veyne, Paul. *Did the Greeks Believe in Their Myths?* Translated by Paula Wissing. Chicago: University of Chicago Press, 1988.

Vlastos, Gregory. *Socrates: Ironist and Moral Philosopher.* Ithaca:

Cornell University Press, 1991.

Vlastos, Gregory. "The Disorderly Motion in the *Timaeus*." In *Studies in Plato's Metaphysics*. Edited by R.E. Allen. London: Routledge and Kegan Paul, 1965.

White, Nicholas P. *A Companion to Plato's* Republic. Indianapolis: Hackett Publishing, 1979.

Index

A

Academy, 2, 27, 29
Anaxagoras, 28, 37
Aristotle, 2, 4, 6–7, 10, 12, 18, 22, 25, 28–30, 34, 42–43, 45, 52, 61, 66, 133, 135, 138, 163, 166, 169
Astronomy, 85, 94

B

Bostock, David, 45, 148–150, 160–61, 163
Burkert, Walter, 93, 137, 163

C

canon, Platonic, 2, 45
Cartesian. See Descartes
celestial spheres, 15
Cherniss, H.F., 31, 33–34, 45, 164
circular motion, 2, 21, 65–66, 68, 78, 82–83, 86–87, 95–96, 106, 123–24, 135, 139, 149–150, 155–56, 158, 161, 162
Cornford, Francis, 2, 8, 9–11, 15, 16-18, 22, 33, 41, 43–44, 48, 51, 56–57, 71–72, 75, 86, 90, 92–93, 131–132, 134–136, 164
Cosmic soul, 70
cosmological. See cosmology
cosmology, 15, 21, 25–27, 29, 31, 40, 49, 53–54, 57, 89, 92, 100–01, 107–111, 115, 118, 122,

128–29, 136–37, 148–49, 158
Cratylus, 65, 126, 133, 139, 166
Creator, 14, 50, 55, 57, 59, 71, 73, 75–76, 79, 90, 130, 143–45, 154
Critias, 14, 17–20, 23, 33, 39, 48, 113, 132, 134, 166

D

Dawkins, Richard, 128, 140, 164
de Anima, 66
Delphi, 92–93, 96, 137
Demiurge, 28, 66–67, 74, 76, 81–82, 84, 100, 132–33, 161
Descartes, 124–25

E

Empedocles, 24–28

F

Forms, 2, 3, 13, 43, 57
Forms, theory of, 10, 12–15, 19–20, 23, 33–36, 39, 41, 49, 51–54, 57, 60, 69–70, 72, 81, 94–95, 111, 114, 118–21, 123, 125, 127–28, 130, 152, 159

G

Gallop, David, 38, 45–46, 146, 160, 164
Gerson, Lloyd, 141, 160, 164
God, 50, 51, 55, 58–59, 63, 73, 75–77, 81, 85, 97–98, 104, 125, 132–133, 136, 140, 144, 163, 165
Gorgias, 18, 77
Grube, G.M.A., 45, 142, 160,

165–66

H

Hamlet, 29–30
Havelock, Eric, 7–11, 17–18, 22, 33, 42–43, 165
Hesiod, 9, 11, 17, 22–23
Hippocrates, 115–116, 138, 165
Homer, 17, 22–23, 52, 147, 154

J

Jowett, Benjamin, 42, 44, 96, 165–167

K

Kirk, G.S., 53, 132, 165

L

Laws, 5, 11, 13, 33–34, 43, 53, 61, 65, 77–78, 85, 113–114, 121, 131, 133, 135, 138, 144, 166, 167
Lee, Desmond, 13, 131–34
Lenardon, Robert, 93, 137, 166
Lesser Hippias, 16, 44, 167
likely story, 15–16, 18–19, 21, 35, 49, 53, 131, 136

M

Middle Ages, 8, 43
Morfard, Mark, 93
myth of Er, 22, 40, 152

O

Owen, G.E.L., 31–34, 45, 166

P

Pangle, Thomas, 13, 43–44, 114, 133, 138, 166–167
Parmenides, 5, 11, 13, 15, 31, 33, 42–43, 45, 53–54, 121–122, 138, 167–168
Phaedo, 3, 20, 36–41, 45–46, 48–49, 58, 62–64, 99, 101, 111–13, 129, 133, 135, 138, 141–53, 155, 159–61, 163–64, 167
Philebus, 69, 147
Plutarch, 4, 10, 33, 43, 45, 168
Popper, Karl, 109, 111, 137, 168
Proclus, 2, 4, 7, 31, 41, 43, 45, 56, 168
Pythagoras, 24–28
Pythagorean, 25–28, 43, 52, 57, 165
Pythia, 92–94

R

recollection, theory of, 7, 12–13, 33, 35, 43, 126
Republic, 3, 14–15, 20–23, 25, 32, 37, 39–41, 44, 47–48, 77–79, 85, 91, 102, 107, 112, 129, 131, 134–37, 142, 150–55, 157–63, 167, 170
Robinson, T.M., 41, 43, 66, 72, 133, 135–136, 168

S

science, philosophy of, 40, 109
Shakespeare, 29–30
Sibyl, 96
Sisyphus, 54
Socrates, 5, 8–9, 11–19, 22, 24, 31, 36–38, 42–49, 63, 65, 69, 85, 99–100, 102, 112–113, 126, 131, 137, 139, 142, 145–146, 148, 149, 151, 160, 165–66,

169–170
Solon, 18
Sophist, 56, 57
Strauss, Leo, 1–3, 8, 12, 28, 33,
    41–42, 169
strong-myth, 8–11, 16, 20, 24–25,
    43

T

Taylor, A.E., 2, 8, 10, 24–30, 33,
    41–45, 48, 51–52, 57, 72, 75,
    91–93, 131–36, 168–69
Tejera, Victorino, 3–8, 12, 17, 24,
    28, 33, 42–43, 169
teleology, 38–40, 48
Theatetus, 126, 139, 167
Thilly, Frank, 118, 124–125, 138–
    139, 169
Timaeus, 1–56, 58, 63–64, 66, 70–
    72, 74, 77–78, 80, 83–84, 89–
    90, 94, 96–99, 101–05, 107,
    113–14, 117–18, 121–23, 125–
    26, 129–170

V

visible world, 2, 15, 19, 51–52, 72,
    101, 119, 121, 159
Vlastos, Gregory, 4, 18, 41–44,
    170

W

weak-myth, 9–11, 16, 20, 158
White, Nicholas, 154–155, 162,
    170
world of Becoming, 2, 9, 13, 19,
    20–24, 30, 35–38, 49, 54–56,
    70, 74, 79, 85, 90–91, 97, 136
World of Being, 2, 20, 35–36, 38,
    40–41, 49, 52–53, 56, 81, 85,
    90–91, 98, 102, 107, 111, 119

X

Xenophon, 26, 32

Z

Zeno, 31

About the Author

John Mark Reynolds is the founder and director of the
Torrey Honors Institute, and Associate Professor of Philosophy at
Biola University. John Mark and his wife Hope have four children:
L.D., Mary Kate, Ian and Jane.